Boo[

Visualizing for Social and Emotional Intelligence

Erin Phifer, M.A., LPC

Universal Publishers
Boca Raton, Florida

Boosting the Mind's Eye.:
Visualizing for Social and Emotional Intelligence

Copyright © 2008 Erin Phifer
All rights reserved.

Cover photo by Steve Visneau

Universal Publishers
Boca Raton, Florida
USA • 2008

ISBN-10: 1-58112-968-8
ISBN-13: 978-1-58112-968-7

www.Universal-Publishers.com

This book is dedicated to my loving husband and
beautiful girls – who have truly taught me the importance of
imagination and emotional intelligence
&
To all individuals seeking the betterment of their abilities
striving for personal success and happiness
throughout their daily lives.

Contents

Foreword 9

PART ONE:
RESEARCH AND THEORY
   1. Introduction 17
   2. Theory of Emotional Intelligence 23
   3. Dual-Coding Theory 32
   4. Synthesis and Proposal for Future Research 40

PART TWO:
DEVELOPING SOCIAL AND EMOTIONAL LANGUAGE
   5. Building the Verbal Abilities 55
   6. Describing the Photo 62
   7. Building Vocabulary 86
   8. Vocabulary Acquisition 90
   9. Identifying & Interpreting Facial Expressions and Body Language 98
   10. Program Steps for Identifying and Interpreting Facial Expressions and Body Language 105

PART THREE:
BOOSTING THE MIND'S EYE
   11. Building the Visual Abilities 124
   12. Imaging a Social Scene 132
   13. Imaging Social Stories and Role Play 148
   14. Imaging Emotional Discrepancies 189
   15. Mixed Bag of Emotions 202
   16. Journaling Emotions 210

PART FOUR:
BRINGING IT ALL TOGETHER AND THE FAMILY TOO!
   17. Family Education and Homework 219
   18. Family Role Play 226
   19. Multi-Cultural Considerations 232
   20. Wrappin' it Up! 238

Appendix 1: Emotional Vocabulary Index 243
Appendix 2: Facial Expression Photos 251
Appendix 3: Social Scene Photos 326
Appendix 4: Social Stories 375
Appendix 5: Emotional Discrepancies 398

Notes 402
References 409
Resources 414

Acknowledgments

My love and thanks to my supportive husband who endured the trials and tribulations of a woman donning the hats of mother, wife, writer, student, and therapist. His consistent encouragement was offered in patience and faith in my abilities. I would also like to thank Patty Biles, my fearless mentor, who possesses exemplary skills when working with children. She will forever be the archetype I aspire to be both professionally and personally. I would also like to thank Dr. Susan Porter-Levy, my post-graduate mentor, for her countless hours of supervisory duties which she performed with energy and insight unsurpassed. Her ideas generated marvelous questions which I have only begun to attempt to answer within this book. I also want to thank my friend and colleague, Ambre Low, who offered encouragement and technical advice whenever I needed a boost of faith and motivation. My special thanks and gratitude extends to the photographers, Alisha Robins Stump and Steve Visneau, who captured the emotions and social scenes within this book breathing life into the concepts I attempted to capture on paper. Their artistic abilities are truly a unique and timeless gift to this program. For further work by Steve Visneau, please visit his website at: http://www.swvphoto.com

Foreword

"The outcome of any serious research can only be to make two questions grow where only one grew before."
- Thorsten Veblen (1857-1929)

As a budding clinician nine years ago, my professional experiences embarked upon the field of learning therapy offering the opportunity to develop reading, spelling, math, and comprehension skills for individuals with learning differences. I did not predict the enormous impact this particular employment opportunity would produce for both my professional and academic careers. While working in a Lindamood-Bell® clinic, I attended Southern Methodist University earning my Master's in Clinical/Counseling Psychology. Coursework and additional therapeutic experience gained from a non-profit counseling center sparked my desire to research the connections between neurological and emotional processing.

Upon earning my graduate degree, I quickly realized separating my duties as a "learning clinician" and "professional counselor" became both personally and professionally impossible. I felt ethically bound to treat an individual in their entirety – be it the neurological processing associated with learning issues, emotional pain experienced from academic challenge and frustration, or social deficits accompanying learning differences. I had discovered my professional niche and quickly sought the experience and education to properly blend these fields.

My work with individuals presenting learning disorders served as a catalyst for the experience and knowledge-seeking leading to the writing of this program. I avidly researched the fields of education, psychology, and counseling hopeful I would stumble upon a program providing a "marriage" between therapeutic and learning interventions. I consistently fell short of this discovery and was unable to locate an appropriate blend of these modalities for treating an individual's comorbid learning, social, emotional, and behavioral issues. The clients I treated required language processing intervention prior to psychotherapy, as they lacked the ability to comprehend traditional "talk therapy" techniques. I desired to accomplish the simultaneous goal of language intervention and emotional intelligence. But, one question remained: "How?"

Although the field has boomed significantly with cutting edge techniques both well-researched and effective, I continued to search for an entity offering simultaneous imagery stimulation and development of social and emotional skills. Therefore, the motivation behind creating *Boosting the Mind's Eye* remained the necessity for an intervention addressing learning and emotional issues concomitantly using imagery and direct approaches.

This program is appropriate for anyone retaining difficulty comprehending social and emotional concepts. The extent of knowledge and skills ascertained within this program rests upon the needs of the individual. If one requires more extensive social and emotional information, this may be accomplished. In addition, this program addresses subtleties and nuances of social and emotional knowledge based upon abstract concepts. Buffering mental imagery offers heightened comprehension of emotional complexities within a social world.

This program is ageless; therefore, it may be utilized (and tweaked) for any population. However, the sample dialogue contained within is written using children and adolescents. This is due to both my clinical experience and personal goal to service younger generations requiring emotional intervention. Yet, issues involving social and emotional knowledge are certainly not limited to children.

Boosting the Mind's Eye has been created for the use of both parents and professionals alike. Due to my academic background and clinical experience, the theoretical foundation of this program has been significantly researched and reported in the initial chapters. However, you will find a great deal of sample dialogue and explanation appropriate for all audiences. I believe in the empowerment of the family system and feel program interventions should not be left solely within the hands of professionals. Without the help and cooperation from family members, this program will not prove as effective for the targeted individual.

All individuals deserve an opportunity to accomplish their dreams and desires. In order to do so, people must possess social and emotional skills promoting successful navigation within their social world. Without rudimentary (as well as complex) emotional skills, people may fall short of their expectations resulting in feelings of disappointment and frustration. Developing imaging and verbal abilities promoting emotional intelligence may unlock an individual's hidden potential promoting social awareness and confidence. Striving for personal happiness is achievable; however, one must possess the necessary emotional tools to accomplish their goals when attempting survival and success within a social world.

Research in a Nutshell

Emotional intelligence (EI) has become a more familiar concept amongst the general population. Its popularity has arisen from books relating the importance of emotional savvy comparable to that of intellectual functioning. The Four-Branch Model of EI (explained in greater detail throughout the book) sets forth a thorough and balanced approach to the importance of emotional understanding and functioning.

However, questions arise: How do people process emotional information? What type of cognitive processing occurs allowing the understanding of complex and abstract emotional concepts? Dual Coding Theory (DCT) set forth by

Allan Paivio relays a dual processing system retaining distinct functions for representing concrete knowledge using images, while using verbal representations for abstract information. More importantly, DCT maintains an additive component of processing, such that concrete information may use both imaging and verbal representations allowing for greater recall.

Can the difference between concrete and abstract language processing affect emotional understanding, and therefore, EI? Emotional intelligence and DCT are further explored offering solutions to impediments of abstract emotional understanding. *Boosting the Mind's Eye* provides a step-by-step remediation for individuals lacking comprehensive development within the four aspects of emotional intelligence. These areas include: perceiving emotions, using emotions to facilitate thought, understanding emotions, and managing emotions.

A Bit of History

Many of the theoretical concepts set forth in this book are derived from the fields of neuropsychology and psycholinguistics. Through the trials and tribulations of pioneering psychologists, the modern era of eclecticism within the field has been created incorporating collective theoretical and therapeutic approaches. Without a combined approach, an individual's cognition, behavior, emotions, and neuropsychological needs may not be harmoniously addressed.

During a time when children are increasingly diagnosed with an alarming number of learning and developmental disorders, neuropsychological research remains a strong and necessary fixture within the field of psychology. Modern Western society appears fixated upon the medical model of disease and pathology; therefore, brain studies are actively sought to bolster biological and chemical evidence used for drug interventions.

Brain studies are vital to understanding human thought processes; however, these studies often evidence biochemical solutions to learning disabilities and abnormal psychopathology. Is it possible the link between brain chemistry and behavior is exploited as a resounding justification thrusting prescriptions down the throats of individuals diagnosed with ADHD, Depression, Anxiety, and other psychopathologies linked to biochemistry?

Current research evidencing support for the brain's language functions demonstrates that individuals may be treated to "rewire" the structures of the brain necessitating additional development. Many insurance companies indicate insufficient research findings disallowing payment for "experimental," "inconclusive," and "educational" services; however, additional research studies may encourage insurance coverage in the future.

Neuropsychological and psycholinguistic interventions addressing language and cognitive development may decrease the number of individuals "requiring" prescription medication for the treatment of inattentiveness/impulsivity (ADHD), depression, anxiety, or emotional issues associated with learning disabilities. When one adequately processes, comprehends, and retains information bombarding their neural networks, their confidence increases, thus appearing less anxious, depressed, and inattentive. Less invasive treatments, such as psycholinguistics blended with cognitive-behavioral psychology, may decrease the number of individuals requiring chemical modifications to the brain. In lieu of adhering a "band-aid" (medication) to the symptoms of a greater issue, professionals can reconfigure neural pathways utilizing multi-sensory mediums creating permanent change for individuals.

Part One:
Research and Theory

~1~
Introduction

Emotional Intelligence

Throughout the ages, intelligence has been classified as a cerebral concept encompassing cognitive ability, logic, reason, and all other "thinking skills" promoting the betterment of human functioning. However, within the last 20 years, the definition of intelligence has experienced a metamorphosis, creating flexibility and inclusiveness within a historically exclusive term. Dr. Stanley Greenspan wisely defined intellectual abilities encompassing more than mastery of impersonal cognitive tasks and analytical thinking historically including: puzzles, math problems, memory, and motor exercises.[1]

In addition, Howard Gardner set forth seven distinct forms of intelligence: Logical-Mathematical Intelligence, Linguistic Intelligence, Spatial Intelligence, Musical Intelligence, Bodily-Kinesthetic Intelligence, Personal Intelligence, and Intrapersonal Intelligence.[2] David Wechsler created numerous IQ scales that are still widely used today within the fields of psychology and education. His own conception of intelligence surpassed his testing instruments, as he believed intelligence to encompass the ability to relate to people, job performance, and overall life management.[3]

Therefore, the idea of what it means to be "intelligent" has experienced an important transition over time. Humans encompass a complex combination of skills, attributes, abilities, mental and emotional processes that cannot be solely recognized through traditional IQ testing. People are more than a mere "cognitive framework" embodying a complex interaction between the logical mind, the emotional heart, and social well-being.

Volumes of literature would be required to discuss the numerous forms of intelligence; therefore, the introduction and foundation of this program are limited to the history, theoretical framework, and analysis of emotional intelligence (EI).

Why is EI an important aspect of human functioning? How does this construct relate to human life and give it the purpose required to conduct further research and inquiry? During the 1980's, an outpour of interest created the platform for the expansion of the term "intelligence."[4] Gardner's 7 forms of intelligence paved a foundation for others to conduct research and create conclusive evidence demonstrating that other forms of intelligence exist. Daniel Goldman published a book in 1995 entitled *Emotional Intelligence: Why it can matter more than IQ*, popularizing the coin-phrase "EQ" (Emotional Quotient) for the general public.

Continued interest in EI has created significant research efforts attempting to uncover and disentangle the intricate web of "intelligence." A compelling and thorough theory of emotional intelligence called the *Four-Branch Model* of emotional intelligence was set forth by Salovey and Mayer in 1990 and will be further explored in the following chapters serving as a theoretical tenet to *Boosting the Mind's Eye*.

Merely researching EI as an academic exercise into the exploration of its theoretical intricacies does not provide sufficient information to those within the practicing field. Although the ideas and research involving EI remain impressive, the practitioner begs the question: How are theoretical ideas put into practical motion creating positive change within the greater population? In order to address this question, a strong research-based theoretical foundation involving the processes within the human mind will be explored providing support for the techniques offered within this program.

Dual Coding Theory

Dual-Coding Theory (DCT) involves the processes within the brain utilized when receiving and comprehending language. One might ask: Why are specific cognitive processes explored when considering *emotional* aspects of intelligence? Isn't the idea of emotional intelligence to stray away from cognitive aspects of the human mind? Although human intelligence incorporates far more than cognitive ability, EI utilizes various nonverbal abilities (i.e. recognizing facial expressions, tone of voice, and body language) requiring specific types of processing within the brain. Therefore, emotional intelligence cannot be fully separated from one's cognitive processing. Humans must continually receive and express emotional language to effectively communicate within their social world, which requires the ability to retain, process, and verbalize an inordinate amount of language.

Individuals struggling with the comprehension of language may retain difficulty with the social and emotional aspects of life. This hypothesis has been formulated from both the professional experience of working with individuals presenting language comprehension issues (i.e. Asperger's, Autism, Hyperlexia) in addition to the study of research relating social issues with language disorders.

Clinical observation and experience have demonstrated

the notion that individuals with language disorders often maintain difficulty comprehending abstract language. Many of the emotional and social skills one must possess stem from abstract, intangible concepts. For example, one cannot physically touch the concept of "love," but must create a mental representation of it to retain and comprehend this complicated emotion. How does one accomplish this? Is it imagined using a symbol of the heart, or an image of a couple embracing? Or, is the word "love" simply retained in one's verbal memory?

Dual Coding Theory (DCT) states that concrete concepts (or entities with physical properties easily imaged) are represented as images, or pictures within the brain, while abstract concepts (or entities with intangible physical properties) are represented in words. Both the imaging and verbal systems within the brain work together creating one's overall language comprehension.

However, what if an individual cannot process and retain abstract language with relative ease? Will they demonstrate difficulty in processing, retaining, and comprehending the abstract nuances of emotional information? Will they image a concrete symbol for love (i.e. a big red valentine), but not grasp the complex and abstract components associated with love because it is a highly inclusive emotion containing subsets and categories within its definition?

Furthermore, what if an individual were able to identify and comprehend concrete components of EI, such as facial expressions and body language; but were unable to adequately perceive, manage, or interpret more complex and subtle aspects of EI? For example, imagine a person with language processing difficulties witnessing an exchange between two co-workers that from appearances seemed to be somewhat congenial (as both individuals displayed smiles and calm body language). However, upon closer inspection, the two co-workers were actually exchanging sarcastic banter stemming from animosity towards one another and the smiles they wore were strained expressions of tension. If the person witnessing this exchange were unable to comprehend sarcasm (which is common in individuals with language and comprehension deficits), they would undoubtedly misread this social exchange.

So what if someone is not able to grasp sarcasm and read social exchanges? Why does this matter? Being a passive observer to social exchange may seem relatively harmless; however, social life does not solely encompass mere observation. What if the individual with language deficits were one of the two co-workers and sarcastic remarks were aimed toward them? Would they perceive this situation as benign, or feel slighted and frustrated because they were not able to understand the verbal exchange?

In order to shed light upon an individual's difficulty with abstract information processing in terms of emotional and social issues, Dual Coding Theory (DCT) will be investigated linking knowledge representation with one's level of emotional intelligence. The reasoning behind the analysis of EI in terms of DCT remains two-fold: 1) DCT rests upon the notion that humans encode and process information using an imaging system, as well as a verbal system. Imaging for retention and recall works best with concrete information, while verbal processing allows for the comprehension of abstract information. 2) Many of the foundations of EI are concrete in nature (i.e. facial expression, body language, vocal intonation, etc…); however, a large amount of EI rests upon the comprehension of abstract concepts (i.e. compassion, trust, love, loyalty, etc…). Therefore, one of the goals of this book remains to evaluate both theories, synthesize the findings, and create a theoretical framework explaining the hypothesized differences of EI amongst individuals.

Boosting the Mind's Eye is presented as a program strengthening EI skills using visualization techniques buffering both the abilities to image and verbalize emotional information with greater efficiency. This program has been created in the hopes of improving upon one's skills promoting permanent change within the brain allowing retention of concrete and abstract emotional concepts. Because the ideas offered within this program do not involve rote memorization, individuals are asked to perform tasks that will allow cognitive restructuring and once accomplished, will create a knowledge base applicable throughout daily life.

~2~
Theory of Emotional Intelligence

Brief History of EI

In order to appreciate the modern scholastic definition of EI, a brief glance at the history of EI's conceptualization remains vital. For two millennia, philosophers have debated the relationship between thought and emotion.[1] For thousands of years, emotion has been equated to the weaker of the sexes (yes, unfortunately, they are talking about women), unpredictable behaviors, and in pure opposition to rational thought. However, the Romantic Movement, accentuating art and emotional expression, as well as the much later 1960's political upheaval (flower children generation; "Make love not war!") allowed for the acceptable consideration of emotional expression. As the conception of reason and emotion evolved, a balance between the two was both desired and eventually sought.

The 1960's political movement provided a timely opportunity to begin publicly deliberating the desire to balance people's perceptions between feeling and thought.[2] Momentum and desire seeking a happy marriage between emotion and reason has carried forth into present times. The current view of emotional intelligence described within this chapter has evolved from meager beginnings blossoming into a comprehensive paradigm of emotional understanding.

Defining EI

Intelligence can be defined as representing the capacity to carry out abstract thought and the general ability to learn and adapt to the environment.[2] The association between intelligence and emotion stems from the necessity of humans to adapt to their environment. Therefore, emotions may comprise a myriad of responses to specific situations, the importance of understanding these "responses" remains vital to the ability to behave intelligently. Subsequently, the definition of EI must involve a broader view of what constitutes intelligence. Varying streams of thought exist regarding the structure of EI. A comprehensive and scientifically validated definition of EI is as follows:

> ... [T]he capacity to reason about emotions, and of emotions to enhance thinking. It includes the abilities to accurately perceive emotions, to access and generate emotions so as to assist thought, to understand emotions and emotional knowledge, and to reflectively regulate emotions so as to promote emotional and intellectual growth.[2]

The premise behind this inclusive definition of EI rests upon the link between emotion and thought. Perception, comprehension, knowledge, reflection, reason, and regulation are all concepts included in this definition highlighting the significance of the union between thought processes and emotions. This definition demonstrates comprehensive inclusion of the main components of EI and understanding each component remains fundamental to the awareness of the effects of EI upon human life.

Four-Branch Model of EI

Based upon the aforementioned definition of EI, the

Four-Branch model of EI created by Mayer and Salovey will be explored and analyzed. EI retains four main components establishing and measuring one's emotional intelligence.[3]

Branch 1: Perceiving Emotions involves the ability to accurately perceive one's own and others' emotional states. Accurately decoding facial expressions, tone of voice and emotional signals (such as body language) allows for competency within this specific aspect of EI. If one is not capable of adequately assessing their own emotional state, they will demonstrate difficulty perceiving and identifying the emotional states of others.[3] Self-awareness regarding one's emotions remains pinnacle to the perception of another's emotions.

Branch 2: Using Emotions to Facilitate Thought includes the ability to harness one's emotional state to become a more creative and effective decision maker. This concept rests in opposition to traditional theories of intelligence declaring that cognition drives emotion.[4] However, emotions are capable of prioritizing the cognitive system to attend to the most important task at that moment, as well as utilizing changes within mood to view situations from differing perspectives.[3] This ability aids human adaptability within their environment.

Branch 3: Understanding Emotions is based upon one's comprehension of the intricacies of emotional labels and categories. Therefore, understanding the language of emotion, in addition to the flexibility of emotional shifts over time, is dependent upon one's complex symbolic representation of emotions. For example, when viewing the continuum of anger feelings, such as mild irritation escalating from annoyance, frustration, anger and leading to rage necessitates the recognition of the subtle shifts within the human range of emotions.[3]

Branch 4: Managing Emotions incorporates one's ability to process their own emotions (without repressing them), as well as the emotions of others.[3] Self-regulation of emotion becomes a vital adaptive skill to function more successfully within one's environment. However, in order to effectively navigate one's emotions, the first three branches of EI require comprehension accompanied by successful execution.

Evaluation and Analysis of EI

The theory of EI has withstood criticism from the research community, due to the surge of popularity among "pop-science" culture. The challenge for research psychologists has been the production of meaningful and genuine evidence to counter wary academics.[5] Main questions asked of EI theory have stated: 1) Can EI be operationalized (or truly measured in a scientific fashion)? 2) Are EI tests constructed with reliability and validity (i.e. are these tests consistent and truly measuring what they purport to measure)? 3) Does EI truly exist, or is it merely an extension of personality trait theory? 4) What can EI predict, and to what extent can these predictions be made? These questions will be addressed in order to effectively examine the theory supporting emotional intelligence.

Operationalization of EI

Over the past 10 years, an assessment measure has been developed and revised in order to evaluate EI as a set of abilities. In the past, self-report measures were used, but have been tossed aside due to the inability to tease apart a person's beliefs from their actual skills.[3] Yet, the problem for ability-based EI tests remains: How does one determine the "correct" answer to a question of emotional intelligence? One method includes the acquisition of norms from a large sample of the population used as a "stick of comparison" for individual responses. Using a large subject pool to compare individual responses is a common method utilized in the creation of standardized tests. In addition to standardizing a measure, one might also obtain responses from "experts" within the field, such as EI researchers, or psychotherapists, and use their responses as comparative measures.[1]

Assessing EI

In 1998, the first ability-based EI test was known as the Multifactor Emotional Intelligence Scale (MEIS). By 2002, an improved and updated version of this test, the Mayer-Salovey-Caruso Emotional Intelligence Test (MSCEIT), was created and named after the founders of the test.[1] The MSCEIT measures eight different tasks devoting two tasks to each of the 4 branches of EI. In order to properly operationalize EI, researchers used norming techniques to compare experts' responses to that of the general population on 705 alternative responses available on the MSCEIT. The correlation between the expert and general population responses was very high: $r = .91$.[2]

The question exists as to whether the MSCEIT is a valid and reliable measure of EI. In order to test ecological validity, or whether this measure can be generalized to real life outside of a lab, researchers recruited college students to watch videotapes of graduate students describing what was on their mind. They found that the college students with higher EI scores more accurately identified the feelings of the graduate students. A conclusion was drawn that people are indeed capable of discriminating between "good" and "bad" responses to emotional problems. Therefore, the responses on the MSCEIT were found to accurately depict emotional portrayals.[2]

Content validity of the MSCEIT has been questioned, due to the dispute regarding the conceptualization and definition of EI. Because the authors of the MSCEIT conducted over a decade of study within the field, the test has proven to be based upon this model, and therefore, has verified content validity of the testing constructs.[2]

Criticisms regarding the reliability of the MSCEIT have been proposed. Issues concerning low reliability among various branches of the test have raised questions regarding whether the MSCEIT is testing these constructs consistently over time. Overall reliability of the MSCEIT is $r = .91$ or $.93$.[2] Branch reliability scores span from $r = .76$ to $.91$. Therefore, the criticisms regarding this measure are not evident according to the current reliability ratings. The aforementioned criticisms were based upon outdated research conducted in 1990 and 1996 that did present lower reliability scores.[2]

EI versus Personality Traits

The MSCEIT is based upon an ability-model of EI representing the interaction between emotion and thought. Other models blend personality traits, skills, abilities, and competencies into a model presupposing EI; when in fact, they remain "hodge-podge" models of neither emotion nor intelligence. A study conducted demonstrates the distinctiveness of the original MEIS from other standardized measures, including the 16 PF (personality trait measure), FIRO-B (test of social and interpersonal needs), and the Holland Self-Directed Search (measure of career interests). The MEIS was found to be distinct from the other standardized measures[5] and appeared to test one's abilities of emotion and thought not accounted for by one's personality traits or personal needs.

Does EI retain predictability?

The predictive nature of the MSCEIT remains difficult to determine, due to its recent availability since 2001.[3] Currently, the MSCEIT is lacking longitudinal predictive studies. Data from numerous labs over the years has been collected using the MEIS and found predictability using the Four-Branch Model of EI. The findings were as follows: Youths with higher EI were less likely to have ever smoked or used alcohol in the recent past; school children scoring higher on the MEIS were rated as "less aggressive" and more "pro-social" by both their peers and teachers compared to children with lower EI; and leaders within an insurance company with higher MEIS scores were rated more effective by their managers than those with lower scores. It appears as though the four-branch model of EI has demonstrated predictability within numerous facets of human life.[3]

Application of Emotional Intelligence to the Real World

As society has become inundated with service industries, the ability to interact with other humans remains a vital component of daily life. In addition, as these service industries require a great deal of verbal communication to function successfully, the ability to verbalize one's thoughts, ideas, and emotions may become the foundation for occupational accomplishment.

Yet, how do theories and research studies regarding EI aid the average human being not involved in academic pursuits? Why should anyone bother themselves with the notion of EI? Through the dissemination and education of the various components of EI, greater exposure may increase abilities, skills, and adaptability within one's environment. Regardless of one's academic status in life, emotional intelligence affects every individual living in an increasingly social world.

Research has found that accurate understanding of emotional expressions predicts enhanced social adjustment, mental health, and workplace performance. In addition, practice alone can be valuable in training an individual in nonverbal sensitivity.[6] Learning to effectively process emotional information provides a meaningful and useful method for navigating one's social world.

In regards to the ability to "train" an individual to accurately perceive emotional expressions, a study was conducted examining the results of two experimental groups. One group of individuals was trained to judge facial expressions while the second group was both trained to judge facial expressions and given feedback regarding their judgments. It was found that the individuals who were given feedback regarding their judgments of facial expressions out-performed those who only practiced identifying the facial expressions. Suggestions for future research gives promise to training programs designed to improve upon the accuracy of nonverbal judgments. In addition, training nonverbal judgments remains a worthwhile goal due to the extensive evidence for the day-to-day value of such accuracy, as well as the recent surge of interest in the perception of emotion given its inclusion under the umbrella of emotional intelligence.[6]

Therefore, through education, exposure, practice, feedback, and interactive training, individuals may improve upon various components of EI leading to more emotionally and socially enriching lives. The ability to successfully navigate one's social world should not be underestimated. If one is not well-adept at obtaining positive interactions and exchanges with other humans, they may experience frustration and loneliness as they stumble through life's social obstacles.

Future Implications of EI

EI will continue to be a "hot-button" for researchers and laypersons alike. The idea that emotions and reason are conjoined and interactive offers a wealth of opportunities for study. However, the question remains: Why are some individuals more capable of encoding, processing, and utilizing the four components of EI? What is it about the human brain allowing individual differences, and can these differences be remediated?

In order to explore the nature of the human mind and its ability to encode language and information, Dual-Coding Theory (DCT) will be explored and analyzed. DCT offers the possibility of comprehending the nature of language processing as it applies to the interpretation and perception of emotions. In order to consider possible training or remediation involving various components of EI, one must explore well-researched theory to create a solid working paradigm on which to base a program. DCT offers an explanation of language processing, including both concrete and abstract concepts, which remain vital for the comprehension of emotional information.

To exemplify this point, if one were to get "stuck" at the concrete level of language processing, how would they process the abstract concepts involved within the nuances and subtleties of emotional language? Imagine an individual with primarily concrete language understanding seeing their friend sitting on the grass next to a tree studying for a test. This individual may be able to perceive a smile as representing happiness (concrete), but might be unable to identify the subtle nuance of a person's shift in mood from happiness to intense concentration. This can be imagined by the friend sitting on the grass studying, looking up, smiling and saying "hello," and then returning to their studies with a look of intense concentration. However, the individual with extremely concrete understanding of emotional expression may misread this shift in facial expression to one of a personal slight ("they don't like me because they are ignoring me, or no longer smiling at me") versus their friend merely returning to the concentration of their studies. This may result in that individual getting their feelings hurt, or responding inappropriately to their friend by displaying anger or hostility.

These subtleties of emotional understanding remain difficult to teach directly. However, if one were to strengthen their imaging abilities, which bolster language comprehension and emotional vocabulary, they may retain more of the necessary building blocks for the comprehension of emotional information.

History of DCT

The seeds of DCT were sown as a theory representing the first systematic approach to the study of imagery and its functions.[1] Before and after the turn of the century, the study of imagery was given importance solely to the functions of memory and thought. However, due to the "introspective" thought process filtering through theories of psychology during that time, imagery research was scarce within North America. Behaviorists felt introspection warped conscious thought and was therefore too subjective. Excluding the occasional article published in regards to the vividness of imagery functions, little research was conducted.

The first publication of DCT occurred in 1971 was formulated by Allan Paivio who took an approach in opposition to introspection in regards to the "vividness" of imagery. Instead, he focused upon a systematic measurement of imagery in relation to memory tasks. Some of the initial variables studied included: language structures and imagery-evoking words; experiments designed to encourage or interfere with imagery; and individual differences within imaging abilities.[1]

Overview of DCT

DCT remains an in-depth framework theorizing a multiple coding theory for verbal and nonverbal language processing systems within the mind.[1] DCT proposes that cognition involves the processing of two separate but interconnected systems - one system reserved for verbal representations and another system existing for imagery representations.[2]

Specifically, the theory focuses upon the symbolic contrast and independence between the verbal and nonverbal substrates. The assumption remains that verbal and nonverbal systems may function independently from one another, with one system being active without the other, or both systems being active simultaneously. The basis of DCT states that mental visual imagery and language are the two key types of representation used by humans. These two forms of mental representations are not exclusive from one another. The significance of mental imagery for human cognition arrives from the interaction between mental image and language.[3]

Basic structures of DCT. The units that represent these two specific modalities (verbal and nonverbal systems) are: logogens (word generators within the mind) and imagens (image generators within the mind). These terms allow for the differentiation between the structural representations corresponding to the specific sensory modality stimulated. The imagen and logogen units are assumed to vary in size, dependent upon the complexity of the information being processed with more complex units being built from smaller ones. To exemplify how this information may be processed, a human body would be considered a more complex unit of information built from smaller pieces of information, such as the head, arms, legs, etc. In addition to various sizes and complexities of mental representations, information may also be processed linearly, such as a word being comprised of numerous sounds.[1]

Levels of processing. DCT proposes three levels of processing: 1) representational processing, which involves the direct activation of logogens from word stimuli and imagens by nonverbal stimuli; 2) referential processing involves the activation across the verbal and nonverbal systems necessitated in order to create images for words, as well as naming objects (giving words to images); 3) associative processing involves activation within either system including the spread of association amongst words or images. Associative processing may be conceptualized as a parallel processing activation in which either system may be involved simultaneously.[1]

The importance of the three levels of processing becomes evident in the activation of the specific system and the transformation of information as imagens for nonverbal representation and logogens for verbal representation. The premise behind DCT states that verbal and nonverbal processes transform and organize information differently. While the verbal system creates sequential structures based upon level of complexity (i.e. sounds to words and words to sentences) and temporal order, the nonverbal system relies upon spatial dimensions (i.e. mental rotations and changes in size), changes within sensory elements (imagined sounds and colors), and movement of imagined entities.[1]

Concrete versus Abstract

DCT proposes that concrete verbal information is more easily imaged and processed than abstract information. Concrete language evokes images within the mind, while abstract language has less of an ability to do so. Concrete words are processed as both an imagen and a logogen, while abstract words are merely processed within the verbal system.[2] Concrete words receive a double "whammy" of processing and encoding within the language system.[4] Because of this increased activation, concrete language creates more elaborate mental representations, thereby making concrete language more memorable and comprehensible.[6]

Paivio (1991) proposed an additive effect to DCT, such that imagery supplements verbal processing. Studies have shown superiority of concrete words during free recall over that of abstract words. The explanation behind this phenomenon rests upon the notion that imagery aids associative learning when relevant verbal factors are controlled. In an experiment conducted by Paivio in 1981, bilingual subjects wrote down the English names of pictures, as well as translated concrete French nouns into English. An unexpected finding emerged, with recall being twice as high for picture-generated words as for the translated words. The explanation for this finding states that the results favor a dual coding interpretation in which the picture plus the generated English word contributed more to the additive effect than did the verbal component (French word plus its generated English translation). Hence, the additive effect of concrete words being processed with both imagens and logogens remains more vital to recall than merely encoding a word through the verbal system.[1]

According to a study examining the neural base of image and language interactions using PET scans, concrete words were more easily recalled than abstract words. When viewing the PET scans for neural activity during concrete and abstract language stimulation, researchers did not find a significant increase in the language areas of the brain during the mental imagery task, as compared to a task using abstract words. The bilateral superior temporal language areas were found to be more active during the abstract word processing. It was concluded that the language areas of the brain are more likely to be utilized when language is the sole source of incoming information versus when both imagery and language are used in conjunction. This finding indicates that the introduction of imagery dictates the dispersal of activity within the brain to both language and visual areas.[3]

Analysis and Evaluation of DCT

DCT has been academically challenged by those in disagreement with the dual system concept of processing language. Some theorists believe in a single coding system, which utilizes contextual clues within language when processing concrete and abstract language. Paivio's analysis of his own theory states that DCT rests upon the assumption that the language of thought is multimodal and relatively concrete; however, opposing theories are based upon the premise that thought is abstract and unimodal, which is perceived as internalized words and sentences. Recent theories have been based upon an amodal structure that is based upon rule-governed computational processes.[1]

Do alternative explanations of language processing retain significant scientific evidence to appropriately debunk DCT? Or, does DCT rest upon firm scientific ground defending its existence? The answers may be found when comparing an alternative theory with DCT and analyzing the associated data.

Context-Availability Model

A major theory juxtaposing DCT, the Context-Availability Model, proposes an alternative view regarding the effects of concrete and abstract language processing.[4] Where DCT presupposes separate processing systems based upon differing knowledge representations (i.e. concrete using imagens and abstract using logogens), the context-availability model is based upon a single-code account of information processing.

This theory states that differences between concrete and abstract processing arise from the lack of "built-in" contextual support present within abstract stimuli. This theory postulates that concrete words are more easily recalled than abstract words because concrete words retain more contextual cues than abstract language. These contextual cues may be found within the subject's knowledge base, or within the stimulus materials themselves. Abstract words presented in isolation require contextual support more so than concrete words because they are inherently ambiguous and more difficult to process.[4] Studies conducted by Schwanenflugel and colleagues found that when contextual cues for concrete words were eliminated, contextual cues became a better predictor of reaction time than whether the word was concrete or abstract.[4]

Kounios & Holcomb (1994) rebut with two issues involving the series of Schwanenflugel's studies. First, they state that contextual cues as an important factor of reaction time may not be due to the separateness but to the additive quality of contextual cues and concreteness. Therefore, providing context for any type of word may create an interaction effect, rather than disproving the dual-coding effect entirely.

Second, in order to accurately state that the reaction time for contextual cues was faster than the reaction time dependent upon the "concreteness" of the word, one must prove the rating procedure assessing context availability and concreteness had equal measurement error, along with equal ranges within the rating scales themselves. This type of quality within the measurements would require specific norming procedures ensuring reliability and validity. To state that the context-availability model supersedes DCT would be inaccurate, as the evidence appears to be somewhat inconclusive. Further research and studies within this particular area must occur in order to be definitive.

Application of DCT to the Real World

DCT offers a wealth of information for those within the fields of psychology and education. Programs based upon Paivio's theory stating the brain processes verbal and nonverbal information distinctly, as well as simultaneously, have already been created and published. One particular program entitled Visualizing and Verbalizing®, written by Nanci Bell, is based upon imagery research.

According to Bell (1991):
> [Paivio] has been attempting to demonstrate the way in which imagery can affect the acquisition, transformation, or retrieval of different classes of information. His dual coding theory for cognition defines imagery (usually visual imagery) as one of two types of cognitive code. The other type is verbal code. Paivio suggested that linguistic competence and performance are based on a substrate of imager. Imagery includes not only static representations of objects, but also dynamic representations of action sequences and relationships between objects and events (p. 251).

Bell used this type of information to create a program allowing individuals to increase their imaging abilities when comprehending written text. This program has been quite successful. In the 2003-2004 school year, Lindamood-Bell Learning Processes® serviced 2,593 at-risk Kindergarten through 12th grade students from 116 schools in eleven states using Lindamood-Bell instruction.[5]

It was reported that 121 of the 819 at-risk elementary students received specific comprehension remediation using the Visualizing and Verbalizing® program during the 2003-2004 school year. These children pre-tested at the 9th percentile for reading comprehension. After an average of 81 hours of instruction, their reading comprehension post-tested at the 37th percentile ($p < .05$).[5] This type of intervention, based upon Paivio's DCT, has proven success when bolstering reading comprehension through the stimulation of both imagery and verbal components of the language system.

In addition, researchers have discovered the integration of instructional text and diagrams to be very helpful for learning. It was found that students' learning became enhanced when corresponding words and pictures were presented within close physical proximity.[7] It appears as though pictorial representations further anchor verbal information. This application is witnessed in many textbooks illustrating concepts in science, history, math, and literature.

~4~
Synthesis & Proposal for Future Research

We are like dwarfs sitting on the shoulders of giants. We see more, and things that are more distant than they did, not because our sight is superior or because we are taller than they, but because they raise us up, and by their great stature adds to ours.[4]
- John of Salisbury, 11th century monk

    One may not readily consider the Four-Branch Model of Emotional Intelligence and Dual Coding Theory conjointly for mutual synthesis and evaluation. Indeed, they each stand alone within the field of psychology offering a plethora of pertinent information and considerations for future research. However, the purpose remains to create a new idea based upon existing theories. The pairing of these two theories may appear somewhat unforeseen; however, the ultimate goal is to make connections not previously considered.

    Scientific research has the benefit of continuing where others have ceased; thereby, advancing various fields of inquiry. Occupational and life experiences, as well as fortuitous events, may provide an opportunity for innovation created for practical purposes. Practical purpose was the driving force behind the evaluation and synthesis of emotional intelligence and DCT. The overall goal of this theoretical deconstruction and reconstruction is based upon future efforts in clinical remediation. Sewing these theories together for the purposes of application to daily life and future research has been attempted through the publication of this book.

The Nagging Question

The question inspiring this book came to fruition based upon years of clinical experience with a certain population of individuals. Individuals diagnosed with Autistic Spectrum Disorders (ASD), including Asperger's Syndrome, Pervasive Developmental Disorder, and Autism, were often referred for treatment because they required remediation in their ability to comprehend, verbalize language, and function socially. Pouring through the research illuminated the reasons behind their need for language remediation.

Research indicates that Autistic individuals present limitations within their use of inner speech, or self-thought mediating the interaction between one's intellectual and social environment. Inner speech allows vital language skills to develop; therefore, if inner speech is underdeveloped, individuals will demonstrate difficulty both using language as a socially-interactive tool and abstract reasoning for logical thought.

Inner speech plays an intermediate role in executive control, which Autistic individuals historically present deficits. Executive control allows for planning and cognitive flexibility. Individuals with Autism do not readily create internal verbal codes coinciding with pictorial information compared to individuals without Autism. Hence, they do not naturally dually encode language. In a nutshell, individuals with Autism do not utilize inner speech, which stunts their language development, abstract thought processes, and overall social interaction.[6]

The nagging question remains: Can we take abstract emotional information and anchor it with concrete images developing language comprehension and overall emotional intelligence? Dual Coding Theory suggests this possibility indeed exists.

DCT offers the scientifically evidenced notion that the brain has two systems for processing information. One system attends to concrete knowledge using image representation, while the other system attends to abstract knowledge based upon verbal representation. Can these dual systems of processing be developed in imbalanced ways within individuals spanning across the general population? If so, can abstract knowledge be broken down into smaller subcategories in order to isolate specific forms of language creating difficulty? Paivio (2007) states:

> We are born with the capacity to image, but its role in the growth of knowledge can be improved by training. Research evidence as early as the 1940s showed that mental images can be conditioned…The interesting conceptual shift here is that imagery as a product of learning came to be viewed as a process that mediates learning (p. 27).

According to Ian Robertson in his book, *Opening the Mind's Eye*, individuals can be divided into "visualizers" and "verbalizers," meaning that some individuals have an innate ability to visualize or verbalize more easily. Albert Einstein was noted to be a "visualizer," as he often solved mathematical and physics equations using mental imagery. However, Robertson states that often the "verbalizers" are the individuals who benefit the most from enhanced development of the mind's eye – adding mental images to their repertoire of words.

Concrete versus Abstract Emotional Concepts

Where within the structure of emotional intelligence does information become dramatically more abstract generating significant comprehension deficits for individuals with under-developed verbal systems? Which components of emotional intelligence are the most abstract and necessitate concrete anchoring?

Imaging and verbal abilities have been statistically proven through research to improve as a result of remediation using the Visualizing/Verbalizing® program.[1] Yet, merely buffering an individual's imaging and verbal abilities does not necessarily create the level of abstraction required to comprehend the subtle nuances of emotional language. Are those who cannot think abstractly destined to lack superior skills within emotional intelligence?

Learning concrete examples without abstract principals remains fragmentary, while learning abstract principles without concrete examples is superficial. Both concrete and abstract language are vital for overall understanding. After all, the term *abstract* literally means to draw out – as one would deduce an abstraction from concrete experience.[5] In regards to emotional intelligence, what concepts infer concrete and/or abstract meaning? How does one delineate emotional information according to concrete and abstract language? A review of the four-branches of EI illuminates various possibilities.

Branch-by-Branch

The Four-Branch Model of EI creates a hierarchy of emotional skills and abilities based upon concrete concepts ranging to more abstract emotional knowledge. By analyzing each branch and applying DCT, one may shed light upon the concrete to abstract continuum within EI using DCT as a language processing guide.

The first branch, *Perceiving Emotions*, involves one's ability to perceive their own and others' emotional states by reading facial expressions, tone of voice, and body language. A study conducted by Pollak (2000) demonstrated physical abuse to interfere with a child's ability to perceive facial expressions. He showed the children within the study photos depicting a range of emotions, such as: happy to fearful, happy to sad, angry to fearful, or angry to sad. The results indicated that abused children were more likely to categorize a face as angry, even when anger was present in only a slight amount.[2] This study exemplifies the strength that knowledge and experience may give to one's imagery representations of emotion.

For example, it may be plausible that one's ability to identify emotional states relies upon concrete knowledge and experience stored as an imagen within one's mind. A baby recognizes a happy, sad, angry, or fearful face early within their development and stores that image for future facial recognition. The ability to recognize a happy, sad, angry, or fearful face is not considered a difficult task for most individuals because these emotions are common and easily identified.

Yet, how does an individual lacking sufficient imagery identify vague, or mixed-emotions? Will an individual lacking sufficient visualization skills retain and recognize emotions on a continuum, such as a face demonstrating frustration to anger, irritation to anger, or anger to rage? Anger may be perceived on a mood elevation continuum obvious to some; however, obscure to others. An individual may begin with the feeling of annoyance, move to irritation, then frustration, elevate to anger, and finally to rage. Would all of these emotions be easily deciphered? If one were to place a photo of each of these emotions on a table, would a person with less developed EI abilities be able to decipher them, or place them within a logical sequence?

The second branch, *Using Emotions to Facilitate Thought*, utilizes one's emotional state to become more effective in decision-making and creative thought. This stage relies upon emotional recognition, which would depend greatly upon a person's concrete and abstract representation of emotional vocabulary. If a person perceived concrete concepts of emotions (such as smile, slouch, shout, waving, pout, kiss) because these ideas are more readily imaginable; but lacked an ability to comprehend and retain abstract emotional concepts, their concept of emotions would be very limited. Abstract emotions may include: respect, honesty, integrity, sincerity, loyalty, responsibility, courage, discipline, commitment, mistakes, denial, empathy, etc. If one does not sufficiently comprehend abstract emotional concepts, how do they utilize their emotions to facilitate thought and decision making?

This is analogous to asking a person to play the position of quarterback in a football game when they don't know the rules and have no experience with the game. One solution is to concretize emotions when defining them. Providing a picture of a person's face and body when eliciting an emotion, including a verbal definition, and using a contextual example facilitates the process of comprehension through the involvement of both imaging and verbal systems. Dual coding bolsters retention of emotional terms because the verbal code is anchored with imagery.

The third branch, *Understanding Emotions*, involves one's comprehension of the intricacies of emotional labels and categories. Understanding the language of emotion, in addition to the flexibility of emotional shifts over time, is dependent upon one's complex symbolic representation of emotions. A complex symbolic representation of emotions would remain difficult for individuals who lack the ability to retain and comprehend abstract information. The idea that emotional continuums are intricate, vague, and involve a large amount of "gray area" remains problematic for individuals. "Concrete thinkers" do not flexibly shift their thought process and emotional outlook with relative ease.

A research study concluded that the ability to distinguish one's emotional states has significant implications for well-being. Participants in the study who pinpointed a specific negative personal emotion were capable of engaging in more emotion management strategies. The implications of this study conclude that the ability to differentiate and label emotions represents a vital skill when learning to successfully deal with emotions.[2]

The fourth branch of EI, *Managing Emotions*, incorporates one's ability to process their own and others' emotions. It has been found that individuals scoring high in the managing emotions branch of EI were rated "more caring" and "emotionally supportive" by their friends.[2] If one does not possess definitive understanding of abstract emotional concepts, will they be able to identify, process, or manage their own emotions effectively? For example, if one does not comprehend the abstract concept of "commitment," will they understand another's frustration when they violate that commitment? Like the inability to play quarter back in a football game without knowledge of the rules, it is similarly difficult to play the "emotional game" without sufficient understanding of emotional concepts.

One study exemplifies how the use of diverse strategies for managing emotions creates alternative physical consequences. The methodology of the study consisted of showing undergraduates disgust-provoking video clips of medical procedures (i.e. amputation). Individuals who were not asked to suppress their emotions did not demonstrate latent physical signs of arousal, while those asked to hide their feelings showed increased pulse rate and other physical signs of arousal. A third group of individuals was asked to view the film objectively and remain emotionally detached. The results of the third group showed lower levels of disgust, and no heightened physical arousal. This study reveals an important physical cost for individuals chronically suppressing negative emotions. However, monitoring and evaluating one's emotions may be strategically useful, as the third group was asked to do when viewing the tape with greater objectivity.[2]

Implications for Future Research

It has been found that children with language impairments (LI) may have a higher incidence of psychiatric diagnoses. Problems with social withdrawal and social interaction may be apparent. One particular study indicated that children with LI may retain difficulty understanding or communicating the affective nuances of language, which may lead to misinterpretation of social cues. In addition, it was found that kids with LI were able to imitate affective speech; however, they may not have comprehended the emotional intent of the words.[3] Attempts at remediation of these children's LI issues in the past may have not been successful, as the remediation may have focused solely upon the linguistic components of communication, while ignoring the affective factor of language.

Studies comparing children with particular diagnoses (ADHD, Hyperlexia, Autism, Asperger's, Oppositional Defiant Disorder, and Pervasive Developmental Disorder) with a group of "normals" would be useful when determining how language deficits affect specific components of EI. Which of the four branches are the most troublesome for these individuals and why? What type of remediation should be implemented to bolster a child's EI abilities? Can this remediation be preventative reducing the occurrence of psychiatric diagnoses over time?

Emotional intelligence research is relatively young within the field of psychology; however, future investigation should include the remediation of emotional intelligence skills. One suggestion for future research involves the notion that some individuals are more adept at dealing with emotional information beginning in early childhood. Discovering *why* some individuals are more naturally predisposed to emotional knowledge may provide the necessary insight to teach these skills to others.[2]

Viewing EI as a developmentally linear model, beginning with the comprehension of concrete aspects of emotion evolving into the understanding of subtle nuances of abstract emotional abilities, may create a platform for researching the development of EI throughout the life span. Does one's emotional development occur within a linear fashion beginning at birth, or do life experiences, knowledge, biological predisposition, IQ, environment, and parental modeling create a "branch effect" to one's emotional knowledge creating a web of EI skills throughout one's lifetime?

Conclusions

The Four-Branch Model of emotional intelligence and Dual Coding Theory have been defined, analyzed, synthesized, and evaluated. The goal remains to offer innovative thinking to future research endeavors involving the remediation and training within the components of EI. Specifically, investigating the divergence of concrete and abstract thinking processes within emotional language may aid those retaining difficulty executing positive emotional skills. Many questions remain unanswered. However, future researchers resourceful in their creative abilities offer limitless possibilities when seeking answers to questions surrounding emotional intelligence.

Part Two:

Developing Social and Emotional Language

Overview

When researching a new program or thought process, the question begs: "What is the big picture of this particular approach?" *Boosting the Mind's Eye's* objective is as follows:

> **To boost imaging abilities fostering greater emotional understanding within oneself and others, while simultaneously training skills essential for healthy social functioning.**

The specific "how" of this program involves the development of imagery abilities utilizing techniques designed to bridge the gap between concrete and abstract language. Through the use of photos, vocabulary, role-playing, verbalization, journaling, and other forms of stimulation, individuals will increase their comprehension of social and emotional knowledge. As their knowledge base increases, they will have the opportunity to apply their newly acquired skills in a variety of social environments.

Why should an individual be able to comprehend and aptly apply social and emotional information? Most people live within a social environment and must therefore learn to interact with others in a myriad of ways. Why not encourage individuals to understand a variety of roles within one's social environment fostering flexibility and appropriate interaction? Through dissemination and subsequent comprehension of emotional and social knowledge, individuals will be more capable of successfully navigating their social lives.

When individuals are incapable of interacting fluently within social situations; frustration, emotional duress, and diminished self-esteem may occur. Social acceptance is valued for many individuals; however, this acceptance often hinges upon one's interpretation of emotional and social information. Hence, if social and emotional information are misinterpreted, then an individual will not possess the information necessary to base their perceptions and subsequent behaviors upon. However, if one developed the necessary skills to accurately perceive the emotional and social information inundated with daily, their behaviors and decision-making abilities will demonstrate vast improvement. By enhancing emotional and social understanding, the likelihood of living a more fulfilled life within a complex, fast-paced social world increases dramatically.

Book Format

This manual was created with the intention of both parents and professionals to read and follow the instructions offered. At the onset of each new task or chapter, theory and research will be addressed to elucidate the reasoning behind that particular task. Then, a step-by-step approach will be offered followed by sample dialogue. An outline of the specific program steps is located at the end of each chapter providing a helpful and quick source of reference.

NOTE: Group and family intervention suggestions have been included at the end of each program step. Because the ideas within this book center upon social and emotional issues, intervention using a group format will benefit individuals as they are more likely to learn from one another versus exclusive one-on-one interaction. In addition, experiential learning offered in a group format provides a socially "safe" environment to practice and hone newly acquired skills.

One professional suggestion would be to ensure that groups remain small (3-5 people) and be comprised of individual's according to their mental ages. Therefore, it might be beneficial to keep the chronological age range between 2 to 3 years for members of one group. One must use their own professional judgment when creating groups, as an individual's mental age may not match their chronological age. Hence, taking an individual's language abilities, behavior, and maturity will be vital when creating groups.

It should also be noted that individuals do not need to be grouped according to diagnoses. Individuals who are diagnosed with Autism, Asperger's, Hyperlexia, PDD (Pervasive Developmental Disorder), ADHD (Attention Deficit/Hyperactivity Disorder), Sensory Integration Dysfunction (also called Sensory Processing Disorder), comprehension deficits without a specific diagnosis, or individuals with social and emotional deficits may all be grouped with one another. The group facilitator should decide if individuals are appropriate to group according to age, maturity, behavior, language ability, etc. versus specific diagnoses.

Some individuals may not be equipped initially to function in a group environment. If so, that person may require individual stimulation with a professional to boost their skills and abilities prior to group involvement. It is not vital that social and emotional skills are "perfected" for any individual prior to group exposure, as perfection is never the goal of any treatment plan. However, individuals who demonstrate extremely disruptive, explosive, volatile, and emotionally unstable behaviors may require individualized attention until they are more aptly suited for a group format.

Overview of *Boosting the Mind's Eye* Program Steps:

1) Building the Verbal Abilities

    - Describing a Photo
    - Building Emotional Vocabulary
    - Identifying & Interpreting Facial Expressions & Body Language

2) Building the Visual Abilities

    - Social Stories & Role Play
    - Emotional Discrepancies
    - Mixed Bag of Emotions
    - Journaling

3) Bringing it All Together – and the Family Too!

    - Parental Education & Involvement
    - Family Role Play
    - Multicultural Considerations

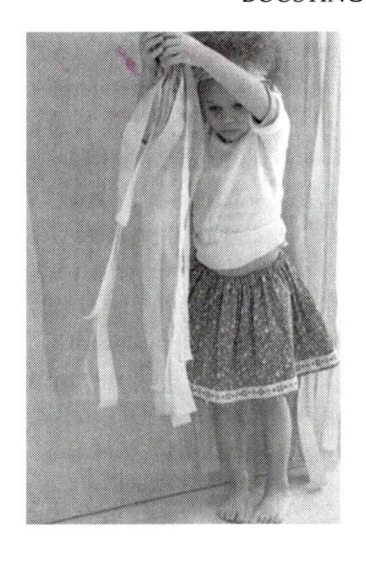

~ 5 ~
Building the Verbal Abilities

The Why's

In order for an individual to successfully navigate modern society, they must possess fairly sophisticated social and emotional skills. The ability to communicate and comprehend emotional language with fluency allows greater achievement to occur within a multitude of environments (including the academic, occupational, and social realms). Our society has become inundated with service industries with communication as a prerequisite for successful employment. Yet, many individuals lack the ability to communicate their thoughts with clarity. Often, their attempts when speaking with another party end in frustration and misunderstanding at both ends of the conversation. Therefore, it is vital an individual possesses the ability to communicate in a logical, fluent, and coherent fashion to effectively interact within society.

According to the authors of *Teaching Your Child the Language of Social Success*, both verbal and nonverbal forms of language remain imperative for social success. They state that only 7% of emotional meaning is conveyed through words. That leaves a whopping 93% of emotional meaning expressed through nonverbal forms of communication, i.e.

facial expressions, body language, tone of voice, and gestures. Unfortunately, a deficit exists for programs offering to teach and develop nonverbal skills. The very nature of nonverbal skills remains complex when providing instruction because our society is primarily language-based.

A society built upon "words" struggles with the techniques required to supply formalized teaching methods of nonverbal skills. *Teaching Your Child the Language of Social Success* offers a comprehensive program teaching nonverbal skills, which is highly recommended to both parents and professionals. In addition to teaching nonverbal skills; however, increased development of imagery processes may create the underlying neurological processes required to retain and understand nonverbal abilities. Once again, with increased visualization follows an increase in overall comprehension.

The term "Dyssemia" defines an individual presenting difficulty comprehending and utilizing nonverbal signals. These individuals often misread facial expressions, body language, or tone of voice, thereby reacting in an inappropriate manner. A Dyssemic individual may be characterized as: tactless, insensitive, lacking in social maturity, retain difficulty recognizing the link between their behavior and the consequences of that behavior, demonstrate inconsistent nonverbal behaviors, and continue a behavior even if it leads to punishment or rejection. These individuals desire relationships with others; however, they often lack the ability to do so. Therefore, the characteristics mentioned above are by no means the "norm" for most individuals, but serve as a reminder that social-perceptual disabilities do in fact exist.[1]

As previously mentioned, not all individuals who struggle with verbal and emotional self-expression are diagnosed with a specific language disorder. Many individuals may never be diagnosed or fall within a neatly defined "category." Regardless of diagnosis or lack thereof, the steps within *Boosting the Mind's Eye* will allow individuals lacking the "complete emotional picture" an opportunity to buffer their social and emotional knowledge. By building one's verbal abilities and self-expression, an individual may feel more "in tune" with modern social and emotional demands.

The steps within this chapter are based upon Branches 1 and 3 of the Four-Branch model of EI. To review, Branch 1: *Perceiving Emotions*, or accurately perceiving emotional states (both self and others) allows one to properly decode facial expressions, tone of voice, and body language, which will be specifically addressed in subsequent chapters. Branch 3: *Understanding Emotions*, or the comprehension of emotional labels and categories, allows flexibility during emotional shifts. In addition, this branch demonstrates the importance of understanding emotions on a continuum perpetuating flexibility and modification of one's emotional state. For example, comprehending the difference between mild irritation and irate anger remains an important differentiation when assessing one's behavior in a given situation.[2]

The steps within this chapter will allow you and your client(s) to "bridge a verbal gap" between one's inner thoughts and verbal expression by bolstering expressive verbal abilities. One of the goals within this program is to amplify abstract vocabulary, which inadvertently increases knowledge regarding emotions and social nuances involved in emotional and social language. Hence, the foundational goal of this program begins by forging a bridge between concrete and abstract concepts using imagery to concretize abstract terms.

As mentioned previously, many individuals are unable to think abstractly, or conceptualize ideas that are intangible. Since emotional concepts are often intangible, it is appropriate to strengthen abstract language when teaching social skills. In order to make this type of language "stick" within the mind, one needs to create a concrete foundation, or anchor for these terms. Through the anchoring of abstract language with concrete images, one may be able to retain the ideas needed to process and model appropriate social functioning.

NOTE: It is important to mention that this book is based upon clinical experience with a varied population of individuals with cognitive deficits. Therefore, it is written by a therapist, ergo using the terms "client" and "therapist." However, it should be noted that this book is not merely intended for those in the field of psychology or counseling. These steps may be used by parents, teachers, speech and language specialists, or any individuals interested in strengthening EI skills. Therefore, substitute "teacher," "student," "parent," "child," when appropriate making it applicable to your needs.

The How's

The key to successfully building verbal abilities requires patience, diligence, and repetition from both the practitioner and the client. By focusing upon increasing verbal skills using short, sequential, and repetitive lessons, you will simultaneously minimize frustration with your client while establishing positive rapport.

Remember to keep things "light and fun" throughout your sessions, as your focus will be centered on your client's greatest weaknesses. These sessions may not seem exhausting to you; however, to individuals with language deficits, they will be labor intensive and require an enormous amount of concentration.

It has been offered that if parents and/or teachers put forth 25% of the effort they exert when refining their children's verbal skills (i.e. correcting speech, mimicking words, teaching sounds and letters) towards improving their children's nonverbal skills (i.e. facial expressions, body language, and tone of voice), major improvements in their children's social behaviors would be witnessed.[1] The purpose of this statistic illustrates the cumulative nature of emotional and social skill intervention; however, some form of gain in knowledge will be evident merely through its direct implementation.

Although the work is intense in nature, attempting to create understanding and elevated verbal abilities in one session will subsequently crush your client's motivation and self-worth. It is crucial to remember that the brain learns best with repetition and in short succession. Babies learn language and motor tasks by numerous repetitions of the same word or movement. It is therefore comprehensible that an individual requires numerous repetitions and practice in order to master verbal and imaging skills.

Through clinical experience, I have witnessed individuals "burn out" when bombarded with the same task repeatedly (within the same session or subsequent sessions) in the attempt to "perfect" a skill. This program has been designed for the practitioner to set a quick pace, while switching tasks within the sessions allowing the client variety and reducing frustration. As a practitioner, it will be important to set a pace conducive to your client's needs, as you will quickly become attuned to your client's saturation point.

As you begin using this program within your own setting, it will be essential to find your own personality and style whilst engaging in these tasks. As you become more familiar with the program's steps and the questioning techniques ascertaining the necessary information, you will slip into a more relaxed dialogue with your client. Following the steps of this program in a stringent fashion is less important than becoming familiar with the style of questioning and building positive rapport with your client. The more secure your client feels within their surroundings, the more expressive they will become, thus elevating their verbal and imaging abilities.

By engaging your client in the processes within this chapter, you will be addressing their language deficits at the source of the developmental problem. Instead of adhering a "band-aid" to their verbal abilities by simply attending to the symptoms of their communication problems (i.e. correcting their inappropriate verbalizations, repeating instructions and commands, or ignoring inappropriate remarks), you will foster the growth of their language capabilities by creating neurological changes within the brain.

By addressing their verbal abilities while simultaneously stimulating their imaging abilities, you will be creating fundamental changes at the "process level" of their language development. Addressing both verbal and imaging abilities is the basis of the Dual Coding Theory described in previous chapters. By strengthening both verbal and imaging systems, you will be building a stronger connection between these two systems of brain functioning in order to improve language and imaging abilities permanently.

The steps within this chapter are followed by sample dialogue offered to reinforce your skills, while providing a basic guideline for the questioning techniques used throughout your sessions.

NOTE: Before beginning the steps of this chapter, the concept of paralanguage must be addressed. The book, *Teaching Your Child the Language of Social Success,* offers an extensive description and steps to remediate issues involving paralanguage. Paralanguage may be defined as sounds which accompany words (or act independently of words) to communicate emotion. Paralanguage is responsible for approximately one-third of the emotional meaning carried forth within language. Specific components of paralanguage include: tone of voice, intensity, loudness, and onomatopoeia (or sounds that are not real words, like "oooh" or humming).[1]

Although *Boosting the Mind's Eye* does not specifically address paralanguage, it will be important for you to monitor their tone of voice and intensity as they speak. If you feel paralanguage requires remediation, use modeling to offer appropriate feedback. If the deficits in paralanguage appear greater than can be addressed with role-play and modeling, please reference the aforementioned book.

~6~
Describing the Photo

In order for a person to identify with their social environment, they must be capable of identifying and understanding the thoughts and feelings of others. Therefore, the goal remains to create understanding surrounding human emotion and behavior, while simultaneously increasing the ability to verbalize one's feelings. This skill will enable an individual to "break out" of their protective social barrier by enhancing their perception of their social world. As an individual describes a photo of an emotion or social scene, they will strengthen their ability to image, as well as both their receptive and expressive language abilities. The following steps will guide you through the process.

Step One: Introducing the Task
First, allow your client to choose a photo from the book. Or, you may ask them to bring in a photo of their family or friends engaging in a social scene, which may offer comfort and familiarity for the client. The photos within the book are designed to promote familiarity of common facial expressions, moods, body language, and social scenarios within a child's social environment.

Sample Dialogue:

Therapist: "Please choose a photo from this section of the book. Choose any picture you like, but do not show the picture to me. Your job will be to describe that photo to me."

Step Two: Describing the Task

Once they have chosen the photo, instruct them not to show the photo to you, but to use their words to "paint a picture" of the photo in your head. Reiterate that they concentrate on the emotional and social aspects of the picture when describing it to you. They may not possess the language required to capture the emotions expressed within the photo; therefore, you may encourage gesturing and modeling of the photo in order to build their social and emotional language.

Begin writing a list of words they have difficulty expressing for vocabulary cards, which will be created later in the session. Allow them the opportunity to describe the photo while listening intently. Try not to interrupt, unless they become frustrated and "stuck." This is an opportune time to establish trust and rapport as a good listener who will not "over correct" every statement they make. Often, the tendency may be to "perfect" a certain term or emotion at that particular time; however, rest assured the client will have numerous opportunities to re-experience emotions and social situations. Consistent practice of these skills will allow for greater comprehension over the course of time.

While listening to their initial description of the photo, try to visualize a blank sheet of white paper in your head and ***only image what they verbalize***. Using this technique will ensure that you do not create imagery of the photo, unless they have verbalized it. Often when learning this process, it is difficult to "turn off" your own imaging abilities, or slow them down to match their verbal description. If you only picture what they express, then you will be more prepared to ask questions stimulating their verbal expression. On the other hand, if you automatically recall and image the photo as they begin to describe it (because you've seen it before and recall it from your visual memory), you may assume descriptive information they have not actually verbalized. This process takes practice, as learning to slow down, or turn off your own imagery can be more difficult than one might perceive.

When first responding to their initial description, you will want to introduce the necessary components for appropriate sequential descriptive abilities. This entails an individual describing the main points of the photo and moving onto the more minute details. Often individuals with language deficits may hone in on a miniscule detail irrelevant to the overall theme of the photo. Hence, you will ask them to verbalize the "main idea" of the photo, or give the photo a title. Then, you may ask them to express certain aspects of the photo that involve: colors, shapes, number of objects or people, background, mood, emotions, body language, action in the photo, perspective of the people in the photo (up close, far away, profile, eye-to-eye), sounds, vocalizations, etc.

Helpful Questions to Guide Verbal Expression:

1) What is the most important or main thing happening in the photo?
2) What title might you give the photo?
3) How many people are in the photo?
4) Can you tell me more about the people in the photo?
5) What are their ages?
6) What size do you think they are?
7) Describe their skin color, hair color, eye color...
8) What type of clothes are they wearing?
9) What is the background in this photo?
10) Where do you think this photo is taking place?
11) Do you hear any sounds in this picture?

12) What might these individuals be saying to one another?
13) What is the perspective of this photo?
14) How was this photo shot – up close, far away?
15) Can you see the whole face and body of the people, or just their heads?
16) Can you see their whole face, or just one side?
17) Which side of their face and body are facing you?

Ensure that your client verbalizes a thorough description of the physical aspects of the photo, but focuses specifically upon the social and emotional themes. This is important, as you do not want them to "hyper-focus" on minute details in the photo and stray away from the goal of this task, which is to improve their verbal abilities regarding social scenarios and human emotion.

Helpful Questions to Guide Social & Emotional Expression: (Modify according to their age and comprehension abilities):

1) Describe the people's body language.
2) How are they holding their arms? Their legs?
3) What type of posture do they have?
4) How does that person's body language tell us how they feel?
5) What type of feelings match that person's body language?
6) Does their body language match their facial expression(s)?
7) What does that tell you about their feelings?
8) What are the surroundings or background of the people within the photo?
9) Is this relevant to the scene or emotion being depicted?
10) Does the background help you to decide what might be happening in the picture? How?
11) How are the other individuals in the picture

reacting to that person's face and body movements?
12) How would you react in that situation?
13) Show me with your body and face what the person in the photo is doing.
14) Do I match the person's body and facial expressions when I do this? (Therapist mimics or models facial expression and body language of the client's description of the photo)
15) Do I match your facial expression and body language when I do this? (Therapist mimics client's body language and facial expression)
16) Look in the mirror when you make that face and tell me what emotion you feel.
17) What should your body be doing when you make that face? Does your body match your facial expression?
18) How should one's body look when they feel [sad, angry, frustrated, happy, jealous, etc...]?
19) I'm going to make a face and do the body language that goes with that face. I want you to copy me while you look in the mirror and tell me what emotion we're showing.

You may need to mimic and/or model facial expressions and body language in order to give them feedback as to the body language they are displaying (or need to display). Using a full-length mirror is helpful because they receive very specific visual feedback regarding their physical body. I often ask my clients to look in the mirror when they model the face and body language within the photo so they actually "see" what their own body is doing. They are often surprised when their body language and facial expressions do not match that of photo. The client is then able to work on mimicking the emotions displayed within the photo. This will be addressed more specifically in subsequent chapters.

Creating self-awareness of one's facial expressions and

body language and the appropriate emotional label remains vital to the process of developing one's emotional intelligence. You cannot assume individuals inherently possess the ability to interpret facial expressions and body language. Likewise, one cannot assume individuals are capable of expressing the appropriate facial expression or body language for a particular emotion. By directly developing this skill, individuals will become more adept within their ability to label, interpret, and express emotions in both themselves and others.

Sample Dialogue: (Therapist and Young Girl)

Therapist:	"Try and imagine that you will be painting a picture of the photo you are looking at with your words. Your job will be to use your words to help me see that photo in my imagination. I want you to describe as much of the photo as you can. Be sure to talk about the feelings and actions within that photo. It might be important to notice the background within the photo, or the surroundings of the people. If you have trouble describing a particular feeling, then use your own face and body to show me. I will help you find the words to match your movements."
Client:	"You want me to describe the photo to you? How should I start?"
Therapist:	"I want you to try and describe the most important parts of the picture first and then focus on the smaller details. For example, see if you can tell me a good title for that picture. Just begin and we will work through it together. There are no right or wrong answers."

Step Three: Engaging in the Task

Chances are, you may receive a *very* abbreviated description of the photo, such as, "I see a hat...some yellow flowers...that's it." Okay, so now what do you do? Well, it is your job to draw the language out of your client by modeling and giving them choices. This may sound like a simple task, but it can be rather daunting. However, this task will prove itself less arduous if you compel yourself to picture nothing, except what they verbalize. Using this approach will require you to ask pertinent questions clarifying their description. The first few times the client engages in this task, it will probably not be a smooth and fluent description. That is perfectly okay. Your client will become more adept at describing and using their language to communicate. Your job is to use questions to guide their verbal expression creating a logical flow of descriptive language.

Sample Dialogue: (Therapist and Young Girl)

Client:	"I see a woman who looks sad."
Therapist:	"That is good start. Would you say the sad woman is the most important part of the picture?"
Client:	"Yes. She is the only person in the picture."
Therapist:	"You told me what the whole picture is about in one sentence. That is really nice. Can you describe the woman so I can have a picture in my head matching the one you are viewing?"
Client:	"The woman has a sad face and looks like she's going to cry."
Therapist:	"I can really see that. Let's talk a bit about her

	physical body first. Should I be imagining a young woman or older woman?"
Client:	"She looks like she may be in her 20's."
Therapist:	"That really helps because I was picturing a more mature woman. Should I be picturing her to have dark hair or light hair?"
Client:	"She has long straight black hair with brown eyes and a really pretty nose."
Therapist:	"That was really helpful. I'm getting a much clearer picture of this woman. Can you tell me a bit more about where she might be, or the scenery I should be imaging?"
Client:	"Well, it looks like it might be really cold outside."
Therapist:	"Ok. So, I should be picturing a big bright sun and lots of green grass?"
Client:	"No! It looks like there are a lot of clouds in the sky. It looks cold because the lady is wearing a long brown coat and snow boots."
Therapist:	"Oh! I see that now. I wasn't sure how to image it looking cold. But, now that you told me more about what she was wearing, that really helps a lot! I wonder where the woman is in this picture?"
Client:	"Well, it looks like she's sitting on the ground somewhere in the city because there's a stop sign next to her and she's on the sidewalk."

Therapist:	"That helps me to see that. I was not picturing her to be sitting on the ground. Good job. You said earlier that she looks sad like she's about to cry. Which would you say looks the saddest on the woman's face, her eyes, or her mouth?"
Client:	"Her mouth because her bottom lip is turned out."
Therapist:	"Can you show me what her face is doing with your face while you look in the mirror?"
Client:	"Well, her face kinda looks like this... (she models a face that is about to cry."
Therapist:	"Your face shows me that this lady is about to cry because your mouth is turned down. You had mentioned that her bottom lip is turned out like in a pout. So, does she appear to be pouting with her bottom lip out like this? (models a pout) Or does her whole face look squinched up like this (models a face about to cry) because she's about to cry any minute?"
Client:	"I guess I don't know what you mean by pouting. She just looks like a woman who was just told that she is really ugly."
Therapist:	"Pouting is when a person kind of sticks out their lower lip like this (demonstrates facial expression) when they are upset about something (writes down 'pouting' for later vocabulary card). So, does her mouth match my mouth right now?"

Client:	"No, I guess not. I think her face looks more squinched up because her eyes are closed tight and her mouth is turned down like the opposite of a smile."
Therapist:	"Good job. I can see that now. You said that that this woman looks as though her feelings were hurt?"
Client:	"Because she looks like she's going to cry and she just looks really sad like someone said something really mean to her."
Therapist:	"Is she doing anything with her hands or body that would show she is hurt by something or someone?"
Client:	"She is holding her head with her hands and is sitting down. She looks like she's going to cry any minute."
Therapist:	"I can really see this now. How can you tell she's going to cry? Do her eyes look as though she may cry, or is she holding a tissue?"
Client:	"She has her eyes almost shut as though she is trying not to cry. She looks as though she is really hurting. I wonder if she has a stomach ache."
Therapist:	"I wonder what type of body language would show us that her stomach hurts?"
Client:	"When my stomach hurts, I hold it like this (demonstrates this motion with her hands by holding her stomach)."

Therapist:	"That's right, if her stomach was hurting, she might be holding her stomach, or bent over in pain perhaps. However, you seem to describe someone who is feeling sad and expressing sadness and hurt with her eyes, lips, and hands. What should I imagine that her body is doing?"
Client:	"She is sitting down on the floor with her knees almost touching her chin. She looks all balled up like she's really upset and is trying to be see-through."
Therapist:	"Wow! That's really insightful. I like how you stated that she's all balled up and that shows how upset she is because she wishes no one can see her. Have you ever felt so sad that you wanted to be invisible?"
Client:	"One time, my parents were really mad at me for hitting my little sister. They yelled at me and I sat on the floor and cried. I held my legs in and wished I was see-through because I knew that Mom and Dad were really upset with me."
Therapist:	"Did you want to be invisible or see-through because you didn't like being yelled at? Or, because you felt guilty for hitting your sister?"
Client:	"I wanted to be invisible because I don't like hurting my family. I was mad at Jenny because she was in my room and I shouldn't have hit her. I felt really bad and wished I could have taken it back."

Therapist:	"You felt remorse, or guilt, about your behavior and wished that you hadn't hit Jenny (writing down the words 'invisible', 'remorse', and 'guilt' on vocabulary cards). I think that we all make mistakes sometimes when we behave, but it is important to know what feeling you have when you are upset. You did a great job with that picture and explained your experience and feelings really well. Nicely done."

Step Four: Trouble Shooting the Task

While you are engaging your client's language skills, you may ask yourself, how am I going to verbalize how they structure their description of the photo in a manner they will understand? A clear method to help clients understand the importance of logical flow might be:

Therapist:	"When you draw a picture on paper, do you color the inside of the picture, or draw the outline of the picture first?
Client:	"I draw the outline first, and then I color it in."
Therapist:	"Right. So, drawing the outline of the picture first helps you to know where to color the rest of the picture. So, when you are using your words to draw a picture in my head, you need to describe the most important parts of the picture first. That is like the outline of your picture. Then, you can tell me the details of the picture, which is like coloring in your drawing. Does that make sense to you?"
Client:	"I think so. You want me to tell you the most

important parts of the picture first before I give you a bunch of details."

Therapist: "That is exactly right. For example, it would be really hard for me to imagine a blue shirt and brown boots if I don't know who's wearing them! Otherwise, I'll just picture the clothes floating in the air. Ok?"

The idea behind the "drawing the outline first" metaphor may seem very basic; however, its simplicity should not be overlooked. Many individuals do not think in this fashion, nor do they speak in logical sequence. However, you can teach them sequential expression by communicating the main ideas first and then fill in the details. This type of verbalization is necessary whenever one tells a story, gives directions, or recounts their day. This type of expression will also aid their written expression over time, as one must often state the main idea of an idea prior to offering details in written summaries.

You should expect this process to require a few repetitions before witnessing dramatic improvements within your client's expressive verbal abilities. Repetition is vital to improving language and the brain requires consistency when attempting to create permanent neurological changes. Therefore, the more expressive practice a person experiences, the greater the improvements in their expressive language abilities. This task will not be the only activity you will be engaging in with your client. Hence, it is important to move along so as not to inundate and frustrate their attempts at acquiring new language skills.

NOTE: Remember that the client should be focusing upon the emotion and social issues expressed within the picture; therefore, do not get caught up in lengthy discussions of irrelevant details of the photo (i.e. exactly how many inches the girl's hair may be, or the particular shade of orange of a person's pants). Get the necessary details to create an image while focusing upon the expressions represented within the photo.

Sample Dialogue: (Therapist and Adolescent Boy)

Client: "The guy is wearing a red coat and looks like he's smiling."

Therapist: "Ok, I can imagine a man in a red coat smiling. Should I image a young man or an old man?"

Client: "He's young and has brown hair. He is leaning against a black car."

Therapist: "Great. That gives me some background information. Let's discuss his face and body more. Would you say that he is showing a big smile, or a small smile, like maybe a smirk?"

Client: "I guess more like a smirk because he has his arms crossed over his chest and he looks really happy about something."

Therapist: "I like how you described his arms over his body. That really helps me to see him. Tell me more about his body. Is he standing up straight, or is he standing loosely like he's relaxed?"

Client: "He has his legs crossed at the ankles. He looks really relaxed like he's just had a great day and is thinking about something really nice. I felt like that one time after I had gone out with my girlfriend, Amber. She and I had

	a great time and after I dropped her off at her house, I leaned against the car and just thought about our time together."
Therapist	"That is a great social comparison to your own life. I really liked that. So, you might say that the man, as well as yourself were reminiscing, or thinking of a memory that brought a smile to your face?" (therapist writing down 'smirk' and 'reminisce' on vocabulary cards)
Client:	"That sounds about right. I guess that would have been easier to say at the beginning."
Therapist:	"That is why we are doing these exercises, so you can discover newer and possibly quicker ways to describe what you see when looking at others. Nice job!"

Step Five: Describing Back to the Client

After the client has completed their description of the photo, your task remains to describe the picture back to the client. This step will ensure that they have not omitted any important details. Also, your description will be modeling the appropriate sequential flow of descriptive language by focusing upon the main components of the picture filtering down to the details.

As stated earlier, it is important you image only what your client describes. Although you have seen the photo prior to its description, try and picture *only what they verbalize*. In this way, you will be sure to question them appropriately regarding any missed details. Once again, you must force yourself to process the visual information very slowly to truly picture the photo as they verbalize it to you. Try practicing this with a friend or family member beforehand, it will help you to "get the feel" for the types of questions you may need to ask. This task will become easier for you, the therapist, the more often you practice.

The following sample dialogue is created from an alternative fictitious story than the previous example. The goal of the sample dialogue is to offer examples of interactions with different aged clients, as well as social scenarios that may be described.

Sample Dialogue: (Therapist and Adolescent Girl)

Therapist: "Your description of the photo helped me to see a couple sitting at a table talking in a restaurant. You said earlier and demonstrated with your face that they appeared to be upset with one another because both of their faces were frowning like this (models an upset frown). You said both were talking and the man had his hand up in the air as though he was really frustrated with the lady. She seemed sad because you stated a tear was coming down her face and she was hanging her head. You said this couple was fighting and maybe they were breaking up because they both looked really mad and unhappy. Did I miss anything? If I did, please help me to picture it."

Client: "Did I tell you that the lady was holding a piece of crumpled paper in her hand? It looks as though she is looking down at the paper. I wonder if it was a letter from him. It looks like she might be really upset by what was on that paper."

Therapist: "That is a great detail! It is often nice to infer, or guess, what might be happening based

77

upon the information given. We may never know what she is truly crying about, but by looking at her face and body language, as well as his, we can make some fairly good predictions. Did you find any of the background to be important to the couple? What made you feel as though they were in a restaurant?"

Client: "All you can see is some people sitting around them at other tables, but it is fuzzy. Also, there's a window and sign in the background. It also looks like a waiter is there. I think it's kind of important that they are in a restaurant because that means she is crying around strangers. I think it would be harder to do that."

Therapist: "I really like how you mentioned that crying around strangers would be more difficult. It is often hard for us to show our emotions to those we love, especially if we are in a public place. I wonder if that made their interchange, or conversation with each other, more difficult because they were not in private."

Client: "I would feel really weird crying and fighting with someone in front of others. But, sometimes, it just happens. One time my Mom got mad at me and I began to cry in the grocery store. So, I went to the restroom because I felt embarrassed."

Therapist: "I think it is great to know what types of feelings make us comfortable or uncomfortable. I also think that by you going to the bathroom, you showed a socially appropriate response to your feelings. You did not want to share them with others, so you gave yourself some privacy. Good thinking."

Step Six: Viewing the Photo Together

Once you have completed your description of the photo back to the client, allow them to show you the photo. At this juncture, make sure they have included all of the important components of the photo. If they have not, it is your job to model the correct verbalization of these missing pieces teaching them for the next time they are asked to complete this task. The most crucial point to remember: *positively reinforce their efforts* first by focusing on the pieces of the photo they verbalized correctly. You will not aid their verbal development by pointing out all of the items they missed, or misinterpreted. An example of this approach might be:

Sample Dialogue: (Therapist and Adolescent Girl)

Therapist: "You did a great job telling me about this picture. This does look like a couple in a restaurant who are upset. One thing I didn't picture was that the woman appears to be twice the man's age. What might be a good way to verbalize to me that the woman is older so that this important detail is not missed?"

Client: "I could tell you that the lady is a lot older than the man."

Therapist: "I agree and that might be an important detail to offer at the beginning of the description because it may affect the main idea of the social scene. Do you think this man and woman are a romantic couple, or could they possibly be family?"

Client: "I think it would make more sense that they are family. So, maybe that is his mother and she is upset by something on that paper. I think the emotions are still the same."

Therapist: "Good thinking. You did a nice job describing the emotions and body language of the people within this photo. It may be possible that they are a romantic couple. How might one be able to tell if they are romantic versus being related to one another?"

Client: "Well, in this picture it is hard to tell. But, if they were romantic, they might be holding hands, or sitting really close together face to face. If they are family, they may also do that, but it would not look the same."

Therapist: "That is great. Tell me what you mean that it would not look the same."

Client: "Well, usually if two people are dating, they look into each others' eyes, kiss, hug, that kind of thing. Whereas family may hug, but they do not touch each other in the same way. It's hard to describe."

Therapist: "I think I understand what you're saying. It sounds like you're saying that when people are a romantic couple, they are more intimate when they touch one another and show more romantic feeling. However, family members may show their love with hugs and kisses, but it does not look romantic. Good job."

NOTE: Try to use positive, independence-building language allowing your client the opportunity *to teach you*. If you try to take a one-down position by asking more questions than giving answers, you will be placing yourself in a situation *to be taught* by your clients. This Socratic approach to dialogue with your clients will enlist their interest and build independence throughout their thought processes.

Your goal is to foster autonomy, confidence, and comfort within their verbal abilities. Feeling confident and independent will promote overall understanding and increase their desire to communicate within social situations. Individuals who feel insecure and dependent upon others to function may be unhappy, as they believe themselves incapable of navigating their social world. Many clients may not realize their potential verbal capabilities pertaining to emotional and social information because they have not encountered a safe and nurturing environment to hone these skills. With your support and patient persistence, your clients' verbal abilities will improve dramatically over time.

Group and Family Format

The following steps are abbreviated and model the implementation of this task into a small group format, or family session. Please reread the steps within the chapter for more specific information regarding the task itself.

Step One: Introducing the Task

Introduce and explain the nature of the task and its importance to overall verbal expression. Ask someone in the group or family to choose a photo from the book to describe. You may also decide to copy the photos and create them as overhead images. You can then put the photo on the overhead and stand in front of the screen, so that you are not looking at the screen while the group describes it.

Step Two: Describing the Task

Describe the steps of the task to the family or group. Ask them to take turns describing parts of the photo. Remind them they will be creating a mental image for you using their words to "paint a picture." You will not be looking at the screen or photo within the book as they describe it. The focus of the descriptions should be on the social and emotional content of the photo; however, they should give enough detail for you to image the social scene with clarity. Be sure to discuss that this exercise is a method for building new social and emotional vocabulary.

Step Three: Engaging in the Task

Ask the group or family to begin describing the photo to you. They may pass the book around and each person may describe a part, or take turns describing the photo displayed on an overhead. You can make this task into a fun game by asking someone to choose an overhead photo from a stack and covering your eyes while they do so. Making this into a fun task promotes group members' eagerness to add "their part" of the description. Be sure to impart the importance of verbalizing the "main idea" first and then describing the details of the photo. Help the group to structure their expressiveness and model any facial expressions or body language as needed.

Step Four: Trouble Shooting the Task

Use choice and contrast questioning in order to clarify the picture. If they are missing a pertinent piece of the photo, use your questions to allow them the opportunity to describe it to you. Be sure to avoid looking at the photo, which offers them the chance to use their expressiveness to create the image for you. Begin to write down new vocabulary words during this process that may require later stimulation for the group or family.

Step Five: Describing Back to the Client

Describe the photo back to the group or family. Be sure to describe it as they did including any omissions or errors they may have verbalized. This is not the time to correct their description; that will occur in the next step. Also, you may consider incorrectly describing portions of the photo to allow them the opportunity to correct you. See if they can catch your mistakes, this will keep their attention, as well as some levity within the session. Be sure to use your facial expressions and gestures to ensure that you are correctly imaging the photo. The more body language you can model for your group or family, the better.

Step Six: Viewing the Photo Together

Turn around and look at the photo on the overhead projector, or within the book. Positively reinforce their description first before discussing any discrepancies you may notice. When you point out any errors or omissions they may have stated, be sure to ask them in question form. For example, "I can see how that lady looked really upset. I wonder if she is sad or angry? Can anyone tell me what type of face she is making?" In this way, you are still playing detective and looking for them to supply the answers. The more you can relinquish your "expert role," the more involvement you will gain from your group or family. Be sure to address any discrepancies that may have been verbalized and ask them to correct their errors aloud. This may be a good time to discuss any emotions or social issues they may not fully comprehend in greater detail. Take the teaching moment and run with it!

Review of Descriptive Photo Steps

1) **Step One: Introducing the Task**

    - Task is introduced and client chooses a photo

2) **Step Two: Describing the Task**

    - Discuss the need to describe "main idea" of photo first, then the details

    - Be sure to remind client to focus upon the emotions and social information within the photo

3) **Step Three: Engaging in the Task**

    - Client describes the photo to the therapist

    - Therapist listens attentively and images only what client describes

    - Therapist asks client to mimic facial expressions and body language in photo

    - Therapist mimics facial expression and body language of client and/or models appropriate expressions

4) **Step Four: Trouble Shooting the Task**

    - Therapist draws out language and description of photo from client using choice and contrast questions

    - Therapist writes down vocabulary requiring additional development

BOOSTING THE MIND'S EYE

5) **Step Five: Describing Photo Back to the Client**

    ● Briefly describe the photo back to client exactly as they described it to you

    ● Check to ensure that you pictured everything they described

    ● Give them the opportunity to "correct" you and fill in any omissions in their original description.

6) **Step Six: Viewing the Photo Together**

    ● Look at photo together

    ● Positively reinforce their description

    ● Discuss any discrepancies between the client's description of the photo and the emotion or social scene depicted using questions to guide their responses

    ● Model the appropriate verbalization of the photo

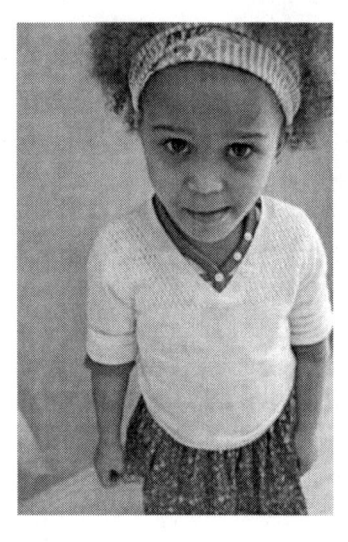

~7~
Building Vocabulary

"What is that word again?"

A prevalent problem found amongst individuals manifesting language deficits appears to be a lack of vocabulary development, specifically within more abstract concepts (including social and emotional terms). These individuals labor with understanding what is spoken to them (receptive language) and/or their ability to articulate their thoughts (expressive language). They often simply "lack the words" to verbalize in a fluent manner.

Clinical experience demonstrates that many individuals retain a larger deficit within their expressive language versus their receptive language abilities. Therefore, they often understand more than they can fluently express. This creates frustration as they are incapable of clearly expressing their thoughts and feelings and may have given up expressing themselves altogether.

When examining how the human brain acquires language, consider how babies learn to understand words prior to their ability to speak. Is it possible for individuals presenting expressive language deficits to have become "stuck" in a crucial stage of language development as a young child? Individuals with expressive language difficulties seem to lack the retention of vocabulary beyond a particular level. Struggling to retain and comprehend higher levels of language often stunt their emotional and social growth, as they understand and express themselves below their chronological age.

According to Paivio (2007), the first words learned by children are object words (concrete), which are named by others. As children develop, they learn to name the objects themselves upon echoing the words they hear associated with the named object. Hence, as parents begin to discuss objects that are physically present with the child, they are encouraging the child to name the object. However, as parents discuss objects that are not physically present, they are prompting the child to create a mental image of the object. In this fashion, vocabulary is built upon as the child develops.[1]

It is plausible that some individuals remain stagnant at a concrete level of language and vocabulary, which may exclude a considerable amount of social and emotional information. If an individual did not have well-developed imagery abilities, they may retain difficulty imaging new concepts. This would greatly stunt their vocabulary acquisition.

Due to an overall lack of comprehension created by underdeveloped age-appropriate vocabulary, a disparity may arise between their ability to understand emotional information and their capacity to appropriately express emotions. The gap between emotional understanding and expression may require specific instruction in order to improve upon their knowledge base. How might this be accomplished?

Research & Vocabulary Acquisition

Research has shown that when individuals are presented an abstract vocabulary term with both a matching illustration (picture) and a verbal example, they are more likely to retain and use the word appropriately than if presented the term with a only verbal example and rule useage.[2] Therefore, in order for vocabulary instruction to be maximally effective, one must include three components: 1) The *definition*, or rule of the word; 2) A *picture* or illustration of the word; and 3) A *contextual example*, or sentence using the word and matching the illustration of the word.

In order to exemplify, one might consider the word "sad." The word would be presented with a definition stating, "A feeling showing one's unhappiness" in conjunction with a picture of a man with a sad face (including a down-turned mouth and possibly tears) reading a letter. Included would be a matching sentence reading, "The man felt sad as he cried and read the letter from his mother."

This example demonstrates the concretizing of an abstract emotional concept. Although sadness is generally a term well understood by most individuals, more difficult emotional concepts, such as sympathy, empathy, or responsibility may be appropriate abstract vocabulary terms, as they are more difficult to grasp. Research has shown that placing an abstract sentence after a concrete sentence increased the recall of the abstract sentence by 70% over placing it after another abstract sentence.[3] By including a pictorial representation of the vocabulary term in conjunction with a matching verbal example and definition, one can ensure that both verbal and visual components of the brain are stimulated with the pertinent information pertaining to a new concept.

Vocabulary Workout Coach

In my professional experience, I have often heard individuals use the word "thing" as a recurrent noun, or "I don't know what it's called," or they may point to objects without using words at all. Your job is to help fill in their "word gaps" by creating a solid vocabulary base. You will often find yourself creating vocabulary word lists throughout your sessions to be used for later vocabulary development.

If you view yourself as their "personal vocabulary workout coach," you will begin to make this process an automatic component of their intervention. You may find it best to stop the conversation and create a vocabulary card, or you may choose to make vocabulary acquisition its own task. I ask clients to make several vocabulary cards at once creating its own separate task, which adds levity to the session and offers them a "break" from the vast amount of verbal information they are expected to express and receive.

The goal remains to build both their receptive understanding, as well as their expression of the terms presented. Once the concretizing process has begun using pictorial representations of new concepts, boosting their expressive use of both concrete and abstract terms will become less effortful because they will have encoded information using several processes within their brain.

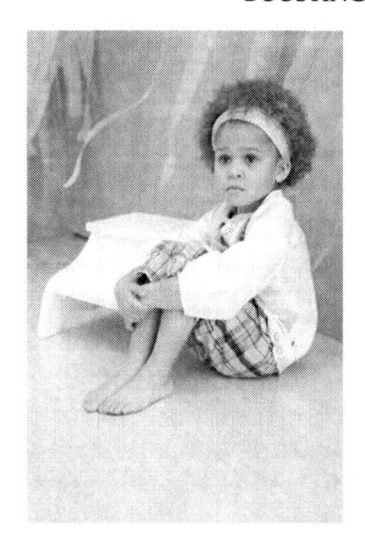

~8~
Vocabulary Acquisition

Step One: Finding the Words

You may ask yourself, "Where should I gather the appropriate vocabulary words?" During the initial sessions, use your conversations with your client to gather any words they do not understand. When you are speaking with them, they may often look puzzled, or have a blank expression. This may be due to feeling somewhat "bombarded" with language. Remember to speak clearly, use age and developmentally-appropriate language, and speak at a slower rate. (I am a natural "fast talker," and initially had to remind myself to *slow down* my language because I was overwhelming individuals who could not process at the warp speed of my mouth!)

Keep a stack of blank, unlined 5 x 7 index cards next to you and anytime they do not understand a word in conversation, write the word down on the card with a black permanent marker. Do not overlook simple concepts by assuming your clients understand their meaning; therefore, all words are up for grabs! For example, check to see if they know right from left, up from down, big from small, inch from foot, etc. You may find large gaps in their language base because they did not possess the abilities to retain vocabulary prior to this type of stimulation. Also, check their knowledge of the vocabulary words listed in Appendix 1 (only the words you deem age and developmentally appropriate) to ensure they have a solid foundation for social and emotional language.

As mentioned earlier, you will begin to acquire vocabulary words throughout your sessions that should be further developed for your client. You will find these words when engaging in conversation and by blatantly questioning their knowledge base of particular terms. Approach this task with less concern regarding *when* it is accomplished versus *how* it is accomplished. You may desire to purchase a graded vocabulary book that gives appropriate terms for each grade level. Many of these lists are also available online. However, your initial sessions will not require such lists, as clients will display a void within certain areas of their language.

You may wish to provide your clients with a large index card box (plastic recipe box) for their vocabulary words. For the younger ones (and older ones alike), allowing them to write their name on the box and decorate it with marker remains a great method for giving them "control and ownership" of their vocabulary box. Stickers and colorful permanent markers are great positive reinforcement of a "job well done!" during each session.

You will need a large supply of blank 5 x 7 index cards. I often write the word needed to be worked on a card and start a stack at my desk while we are speaking. This ensures that I do not overlook any missed terms and that we will work on that particular word at a later time.

Step Two: Vocabulary Creation Process

Appendices 2 and 3 offer a wide range of emotions captured in photographs. This may be a great place to begin acquiring vocabulary (in addition to Appendix 1: Emotional Vocabulary Index). When asked to determine a particular expression in *Chapter 6: Describing the Photo*, they may have been unable to accurately define it. Therefore, use this opportunity to make a copy of this photo and create a vocabulary card out of it. You may ask them to cut the photo and glue it onto the card and to write the definition and sentence for that particular emotion on the opposite side of the card.

In addition to the photos within this book, ask your client to cut out photos from magazines depicting emotions and social scenarios creating a fun alternative to capturing emotional expressions. Adolescents and adults enjoy using popular magazines displaying movie stars because they recognize these individuals and it creates a heightened interest in the task.

On the back of the index card, separate the card into two sections. Within one section, you may write the definition of the word to save time, or have the client use the dictionary and write the definition, if that remains a skill requiring further development. Regardless, you will be responsible for overseeing and editing the definition ensuring that it is succinct, uses simplistic language, and captures the word being expressed. Obviously, the goal is to use less complex wording within the definition than the word being defined.

In the other section of the card, have the client write a sentence correctly using the word in order to create more clarification. It might be helpful to have the client use the celebrity's name in the sentence, or to have them come up with an example of a personal experience using that vocabulary word. Either way, it is important that the sentence correctly capture the meaning of the word as expressed in the photo. In this way, the client will be anchoring the word to a concrete example, which should enable them to recall it with greater ease. Some examples of this would be to use "I feel..." statements, or "Mary/Bob feels..." statements. The client may choose to give that particular character within the photo a feeling statement. For example, if the photo depicts Tom Cruise smiling brightly at his wife, the sentence may read: "Tom feels happy when he spends time with his wife."

If you cannot find the proper photo or cut-out to adequately express the word, the client may draw a picture of their own. Be sure the client creates a sentence that describes the picture, while also using the vocabulary word correctly to ensure the image anchors the word (concretizing the abstract concept). In addition, the client may use "I feel…" or "He/she feels…" statements describing the emotion and picture. For example, if the client draws a picture of a little girl hanging her head with people around her laughing, the sentence might read: "She felt embarrassed when all of her classmates laughed at her."

Once the card is completed, ask your client to take a moment to image the photo in their head without looking at the card. Ask them to recite the sentence to you. This will further anchor these images within their mind's eye.

Step Three: Vocabulary Quizzing

Once the vocabulary card has been completed, place it in the "vocabulary box" for later checking. You may decide to create this vocabulary exercise as its own task and have the client complete several of these cards per session. During subsequent sessions, allot a specific amount of time to "check" vocabulary cards created in previous sessions. Your role in checking the cards means you will be asking the client to recall their images and verbalize a definition or correct example of the word (which is a receptive check of the word). Or you may give them the definition and ask them to express the word (an expressive check of the word). If appropriate or necessary, you may also ask them to express the emotion with their face and body while looking in a mirror. Finally, ask them to use the word in a sentence in order to ensure complete comprehension of the term.

By quizzing the client on these words over a period of time, you will be further anchoring images to words. If the client makes an error when giving the definition, or when expressing the word, show them the photo on the card. Review their definition and sentence with them. Turn the card over and ask them to quickly describe the photo or picture drawn to make certain they are imaging the illustration. The reason behind all of the "checking" and "quizzing" is to ensure they are truly imaging the vocabulary term and can properly comprehend and express the word.

It is important that you check both receptive and expressive uses of the word in order to enhance both sets of skills. In order for an individual to have truly incorporated a new word into their "word bank" they should be able to image an example of the word, verbalize the correct definition of a word, use the word properly in a sentence, and express the word if given the definition over the course of several sessions until it becomes automatic. You may decide to incorporate a "graduation ceremony" for words that become automatic by using stickers or another special form of positive reinforcement for your client.

NOTE: Correct receptive use of a word is when they hear the word and reply with the correct definition or usage of the word. Correct expressive use of a word is when they are given the definition and they are able to verbalize the word. Think of receptive and expressive in terms of the vocabulary word itself. When they "receive the word" and must give the definition, this is considered a "receptive check" of that vocabulary word. When they are asked to "express the word" once the definition has been verbalized to them, then this is considered an "expressive check" of that vocabulary term.

Group and Family Format

Step One: Vocabulary Acquisition

Begin to write down a list words throughout your sessions requiring additional development. If someone within the family or group does not understand a concept, do not brush over it. Instead, take the time to briefly discuss the word's meaning and write it down to be further stimulated during a specific vocabulary task. Ask the group and family members if there are any words or concepts they find confusing and add these to the list.

Step Two: Vocabulary Creation Process

Have the group and/or family cut out photos from magazines and newspapers (or create their own drawings) to depict emotions or social scenarios requiring further comprehension.

This can be a fun group assignment, as it is a "break" from the heavier social and emotional tasks requiring role playing and expressiveness. If desired, allow the members of the group or family to draw their own emotional depictions, or have one "group card" for the entire group. The idea remains to construct a concrete image of abstract information. Therefore, using photos or drawings that match the emotion remains important.

Have the group or family glue the photo to one side of the 5 x 7 card (poster board works well for groups). The other side of the card should be used to define the word. You should supply the definition, or have the group create a definition (with your revision as needed) in order to create consistency amongst the group.

Discuss the definition and any questions that may arise. Allow each member of the group the opportunity to create their own feeling statement regarding the word. You may use a "Round Robin" approach and go around the circle having each person verbalize their own sentence.

Or, you may choose to have one person within the

group write a sentence on the card that correctly uses the word and describes the picture. Or, create one "group sentence" together with input from the members as to the agreed upon sentence for the vocabulary word. Have each member put their vocabulary words in their own special box to be worked in later sessions, or create one "group vocabulary box" to be used by all.

Step Three: Vocabulary Quizzing

Throughout subsequent sessions, check the group or family's imagery, comprehension, and retention of vocabulary words. Quiz the group by stating the word and asking for a definition or the word in context (receptive practice). Or, give the group the definition and see if they can verbalize the matching word (expressive practice). It is important to ensure that the group has both receptive and expressive comprehension of the terms and are making appropriate mental images.

Review of Vocabulary Steps

1) **Step One: Vocabulary Acquisition**

   - Accumulate words requiring further clarification and expressive use for the client. Make a list, or write the words on index cards throughout the sessions. Be sure to make this a consistent and continual task throughout all sessions.

2) **Step Two: Vocabulary Creation Process**

   - Use photos from manual, magazine cut outs, or drawings to depict emotions requiring defining and affix to a blank 5 x 7 index card. Define the word on the back of the card. Use "I feel" or "He/She feels" statements that match the picture and further explain the emotion being expressed.

3) **Step Three: Vocabulary Quizzing**

   - Check imagery, comprehension, and retention of vocabulary words throughout subsequent sessions. Have client define word, use it in a sentence, and/or model the expression. Ensure client has both receptive and expressive understanding of the terms and is properly imaging the emotion expressed.

~9~
Identifying & Interpreting Facial Expressions & Body Language

A Bit of Discussion Regarding Language Issues

Individuals demonstrating difficulty with various aspects of EI may struggle with the identification and recognition of behavior within their social world. Those who retain weakness comprehending abstract information, or have difficulty imaging concepts within the mind's eye, may not process stimuli in its entirety throughout their environment. Their world may consist of a "social bubble" existing because of their limitation in the absorption of social and emotional information. The result of their restricted retention and comprehension of social information reveals one processing mere bits and pieces of incoming stimuli and lacking the "big picture" in life. In addition, if an individual is only capable of comprehending fragmented social information; misperception of social cues, facial expressions, and body language ensues resulting in defensive and frustrated behaviors.

You may have observed an individual lacking the greater social picture when listening as they recount a social story or event within their life. They may verbalize feeling insulted or affronted and you cannot comprehend how or why they perceive another's comments as such. This may be due to their misperception of communication, or language barrier disallowing complete processing of a person's verbalizations. My clients have often discussed that someone gave them a "dirty look," or "always picks on me," or "just doesn't understand me."

Their words are truthful. Often, these individuals are misunderstood and likewise, misunderstand others. One might imagine verbal and nonverbal communication between themselves and others traveling on completely alternative wavelengths, thus they are misreading others and their own behaviors are likewise misread. The final result of this mismatched communication may be: frustration, anger, social withdrawal, social banishment, depression, anxiety, and loss of hope.

Many times when a new client is referred to me for treatment of ADHD, I hear stories from parents describing their children as individuals who "do not listen, have negative attitudes, ignore their parents, 'space out' in class, make poor decisions, do not follow directions, do not understand what they are told, etc." Over the years, I have learned to hear little alarm bells in my brain alerting me to these "difficult children" when they are presented in this fashion.

Upon further assessment and clinical interview of the child, I may find that the child is not truly ADHD per se, but retains a language disorder that may have gone unnoticed. Often times these children suffer from Hyperlexia (poor reading comprehension with a myriad of social issues), or another form of a mixed receptive/expressive language disorder. Not *all* children showing symptoms of ADHD are misdiagnosed. Many fit the diagnosis and perform well with medication and further treatment. However, parents, teachers, and professionals may often "miss" kids who *can attend* to their environment, but *don't do it all of the time*. It is appears as though they are mentally checking "in and out" throughout the day.

These children cannot process and retain the amount and speed of information with which they are bombarded throughout their life. They cannot fully comprehend class lectures, note taking, homework, or parent's oral directions because they are not creating sufficient images within their mind's eye to anchor language to understanding. They may not remember what they learned in school from week to week, follow directions in their entirety, and/or "zone out" in class. Basically, they cannot keep pace with the rapid rate of language entering their auditory senses.

In addition to their difficulty perceiving language, these individuals may not express themselves with fluidity. They may recount a portion of the story, or tell the story out of logical order. They often lack flow within their speech, as well as age-appropriate vocabulary evidenced by their use of words expected for children chronologically younger.

It is therefore comprehensible that these individuals may struggle with social and emotional issues, such as misreading facial expressions and body language. Because they lack the language and ability to image concepts thoroughly within their mind's eye, their social development is often delayed.

Diagnoses and Individualized Skills

All of the aforementioned issues are indeed individualized. One person may possess a few or all of the symptoms described. It is always wise to view your client as a fingerprint, with divergent behaviors and characteristics exhibited in a plethora of ways.

I often verbalize this statement to parents who ask me to outline certain expectations for their child's behavior or abilities based upon their specific diagnosis. "What abilities *should* my child have when diagnosed with [ADHD, Dyslexia, Hyperlexia, Asperger's, High Functioning Autism, etc...]?" I always feel a bit pressured by this question because individuals' abilities are not based upon a given diagnosis. A person's brain is synonymous to a spider web, with a multitude of neural networks created due to one's experience, genetics, education, and nurturing. Hence, it is difficult to provide a blanketed statement regarding one's abilities based upon a specific diagnosis.

A diagnosis is contingent upon a myriad of symptoms, behaviors, and manifestations that may not all be present within an individual. Therefore, my answer to their question often states, "Your child's abilities are based upon their desire, motivation, and expectations they hold for themselves." This allows my parents to realize that a child's progress often depends upon their own desire to improve upon their skills. These skills cannot be forced upon any individual, regardless of age. If a person displays severe symptoms of depression or anxiety, tending to their social perception is not the immediate and necessary course of action. An individual who manifests signs of severe depression and/or anxiety should have these issues addressed first and foremost.

A child's abilities may be predicted with *some* accuracy based upon their mental age, developmental level, past history, diagnosis, etc. Yet, this will remain a prediction and never a recommendation set in stone. The overall goal remains to foster positive rapport with the entire family creating an environment of care, learning, and understanding allowing the child the opportunity to blossom.

I am of the mindset that a person must own their own desire for improvement. In this way, full cooperation will be established at the onset of therapy. With an open mind and a desire to receive help, an individual may proceed to improve upon their skills. When children are empowered and given the opportunity to *choose* to attend therapy and make personal improvements, they will often set their own level of expectation (sometimes higher than that of their parents) and make tremendous gains. I have witnessed this transformation on many occasions.

I feel it is imperative to give children the credit and respect to own their own treatment process. They have often surprised me over the years in their commitment and dedication to improve upon their skills.

Back to Body Language and Facial Expressions

The Four-Branch model of EI provides the necessary understanding regarding the importance one must place upon the interpretation of facial expressions and body language to successfully live in our social world. Branch 1, the *Perception of Emotions*, requires an individual to accurately perceive their own and others' emotional states. In order to accomplish this feat with success, one must identify and understand nonverbal emotional language transpiring around them.

The foundation of emotional interpretation involves the ability to read basic emotions when viewing facial expressions and body language. The ability to effectively read and produce appropriate facial expressions remains pinnacle to social understanding. This skill may be one of the most important nonverbal abilities an individual possesses, as the human face is the gateway to emotional information.[1]

Children are typically able to read happy faces; however, it has been found that some children display difficulty when deciphering an angry versus a sad face. This lack of differentiation creates an emotional discrepancy, as that child may not realize whether they are responding to anger or sadness. Likewise, it has been found that some children lack an ability to create alternative facial expressions when asked to depict a certain mood. These children's faces look very similar when attempting to demonstrate happiness, anger, sadness, and fear.

 In a study conducted with 1,000 children, it was found that between 7 and 10 percent had significant difficulty in either reading or producing specific emotional expressions. In addition, between 7 and 10 percent of the children displayed extreme proficiency and needed no further work in this area. These numbers indicate that approximately 80 percent of children are capable of communicating appropriately using facial expressions, but may require additional improvement.[1]

As you recall from a previous section, Dyssemics are individuals struggling with the ability to comprehend nonverbal components of social language. They manifest an extreme lack of knowledge in the ability to understand facial expressions, body language, and tone of voice.[1]

My assertion remains that individuals possess varying degrees of competence within this area. Some people are "human barometers" capable of reading not only body language, but subtle nuances of emotional and social behavior. However, some individuals lack this ability and fall at the other end of the spectrum, struggling to determine why a person may have looked at them in a particular way.

Like IQ and cognitive ability, I believe that EI falls along a bell-curve, where the majority of people fall within the middle. They are able to read others in order to function, but may have some difficulties within more specific areas of EI. Therefore, this portion of the manual may not prove as helpful to individuals falling in the middle of the "EI bell-curve" because they are able to identify facial expressions and body language. However, like any other skill, a bit of fortification never hurts.

Individuals who fall at the lower end of the spectrum in terms of their abilities to "read others" may experience frustration, confusion, isolation, and engage in inappropriate social behaviors. These behaviors are *not* understood as awkward or inappropriate by the individual who does not have a social "measuring stick" with which to compare their behaviors. Often parents or teachers will state, "I have told her over and over not to stare at strangers and stand too close to people, but she just doesn't seem to understand."

The error in this statement is that the child hears the information, but does not have the current capacity to view their behaviors as awkward in comparison to others. In order for that process to take place, an individual has to be able to store and image the "appropriate behaviors" before making a comparison. In other words, the information received for so many years regarding the correct behavior, or social grace, may have not been retained or comprehended fully within the child's mind. Without the ability to comprehend abstract concepts, such as emotions and social nuances, a person may not be able to compare what is considered socially appropriate versus socially inappropriate behaviors. Therefore, they do not understand *why* that behavior is considered inappropriate; thus, why should they bother to change it?

Moving Forward

If one is to successfully function within their social environment, the importance of identifying and expressing appropriate facial expressions and body language cannot be overstated. By practicing appropriate and varied facial expressions along with coordinating body language, these individuals will create a foundation of "social knowledge" from which to draw upon. By building their concept imagery, or ability to visualize, new facial expressions or body language taught directly will be retained and incorporated into their social schema. Stimulating the ability to comprehend abstract emotions by concretizing concepts with imagery will replace preexisting erroneous connections between emotion and behavior.

~10~
Program Steps for Identifying & Interpreting Facial Expressions & Body Language

Step One: Introduction and Finding the Pictures

To create exposure, clarity, and imagery of numerous facial expressions, body language, and the associated emotions, photos depicting real people and social scenes should be used. The more varied and numerous the photos, the greater the exposure when bolstering one's social vocabulary. You may choose to utilize the included photos in the appendices of this book, or draw upon other photos you have collected. Magazines portraying famous stars and pop culture often capture an array of facial expressions and body language. By presenting a wide variety of photos (with the inclusion of individuals from all walks of life) along with a detailed explanation of the emotion(s) depicted within the photo, the therapist will help the client to identify the emotional expression illustrated.

NOTE: Some of the facial expressions and emotions portrayed within the photos in this book may seem ambiguous or difficult to identify. Their inclusion was purposeful to stimulate conversation and deliberation over the type of emotion one may interpret for that particular facial expression and body language. In addition, you or your client may disagree with the label I have chosen for a particular photo (or category in which I have placed it in the appendices). That is completely acceptable as long as an individual is able to verbalize their opinion regarding that emotion. I will state; however, that blatantly expressed emotions should not be open for interpretation, as they are clearly demonstrating a particular emotional context.

This program step also proves to be an excellent time to build emotional vocabulary. Once a few facial expressions have been explored with the photos, the therapist should model these expressions for the client. The client should then mimic the therapist's facial expressions and use a mirror to check their own expressions. A full-length mirror works best for this task, as often the entire body becomes involved in emotional expression.

By using the mirror as a form of visual feedback, the client will not only be able to "feel" the facial expression using their facial muscles, but will also receive visual confirmation of their expression through the comparison of their expression to that of the therapist's.

Clients should be asked to explore the emotion this facial expression elicits while they perform this exercise. They may be surprised to feel sad, angry, or happy as they perform the coordinating expressions matching the emotion. The premise behind this type of deliberate and concrete processing is to create both visual and motor feedback for the client. By processing this information using numerous sensory inputs, the client will build a greater mental image through practice and exposure. Once the image of that particular emotion or behavior has been firmly and correctly set, it will create faster processing speed for the client as they make social and emotional interpretations.

Sample Dialogue: (Therapist and Adolescent Girl)

Therapist: "Ok, now that we've described some photos and created vocabulary, let's look at pictures of social scenes together. I want to expose you to a lot of different emotions and social situations. I think this will be a great way to build upon what you already know and to learn about emotions you may not be as familiar with. I have a lot of pictures in this book and I've also brought along some magazines to look at. You may be familiar with some of these magazines, as they have a lot of movie stars in them. I thought it might be fun to look at those magazines together."

Client: "That sounds easy to me. Let's see what you have."

NOTE: At this point, the client and therapist may browse through the photos and briefly discuss what they see. Asking the client what type of emotion is displayed and why the characters within the photo are using their body and face in a particular way may be helpful.

The therapist can create vocabulary cards as they go, in case the client is unable to identify or understand the social scenario or emotions displayed in the picture. This introductory time is merely providing exposure leading up to the next task. It should be light, fun, and used to build rapport. Trust will be vital for the next task, as the client will be asked to act out social situations with the therapist. This may prove somewhat embarrassing; therefore, they should feel comfortable while in your presence. Your client's level of comfort and rapport may take more than one session to build.

Work at your client's pace. After all, the client is seeing you to improve upon their social and emotional understanding. Rushing and hurrying through the tasks may create anxiety. You may find that the first few sessions seem to move a bit slowly, that's perfectly alright. As time progresses, the tasks will fly by with greater ease as their skill base improves and they become more comfortable in their new emotional understanding. As a therapist, you are helping the client to further develop the building blocks of emotional intelligence by boosting their verbal and imaging abilities. Once created, these processes will serve as a foundation for retention and greater understanding.

Step Two: Therapeutic Modeling

Once a few facial expressions and social scenes are introduced and a good rapport has been established, the therapist should choose a particular emotion or social scenario from which to work. The therapist may model the appropriate body language associated with the particular facial expression, or emotion being discussed. The therapist should "act out" these movements and associated emotions in order to effectively model the body language for the client. The client is then encouraged to stand up with the therapist and mimic the body language and expressions being modeled.

Through this type of physical stimulation, the client will be able to feel the body movements associated with the coordinating facial expressions, while receiving visual feedback from the mirror. A full-length mirror should be incorporated in this process in order for the client to "check" their body language and expressions with that of the therapist's. The therapist may directly guide the client to check to see if their body language matches that of the therapist's by stating, "When you see your arms up in the air that way, does that match my arms?" This type of direct feedback from the mirror and the therapist will provide the client with a clearer understanding of their own bodily movements.

Also, the client should be encouraged to put language to

their movements and facial expressions throughout this exercise to attach meaning to their actions. This will aid their understanding of the importance of body language and facial expressions when showing or interpreting emotion. For example, if showing frustration or impatience, the therapist may model their hand on their hips and have the client match their movements whilst verbalizing that often hands may go on their hips when showing frustration or impatience. In addition, they may verbalize their frown or associated facial expression with the body language.

This is merely another method for processing emotional information through a variety of sensory inputs. By incorporating motor (haptic), visual, and auditory feedback, the client processes information through numerous modalities creating additional reinforcement within the neural networks of the brain. With greater experience and reinforcement, these concepts will become more firmly linked to one another within their neural web.

Sample Dialogue: (Therapist and Young Boy)

Therapist: "I was hoping to try something a little different. We've been looking through photos and magazines and talking about the body language and faces people make when they feel certain things. I also think that it's really important to practice some of these in order for us to feel them. So, why don't we start with this picture of the woman who is smiling and grabbing the little girl's arm? What do you think is going on in this picture?"

Client: "Well, I think it is a mom and a daughter just by the way they are acting with each other. The lady is smiling, but the girl is crying. So, maybe the mom is happy and the girl is sad."

Therapist:	"That's a great start. I would agree that these two look like a mother and daughter pair. Also, the little girl does look sad. Can you tell me more about her body language that may tell us that she might be feeling something more than sadness?"
Client:	"It looks like she's screaming and throwing her arms in the air. So, maybe she's mad?"
Therapist:	"That's great! I was thinking that also. What about the mom? Do you think that she's happy?"
Client:	"Well, at first I thought she was happy because she was smiling really big. But, it looks like she's holding on really tight to her daughter's arm to keep her from falling on the floor. So, she doesn't seem that happy. Her eyes look like they are looking away – maybe she's looking for someone?"
Therapist:	"I agree. Even though she is smiling, her body is telling a different story. I think it might be hard to be happy when your child is upset. I like how you noticed her eyes looking away from her daughter. Tell me more about the rest of her body."
Client:	"Well, her legs are really straight like she's trying not to fall over as she holds her kid's arm. Her purse is hanging down by her hand, like maybe it fell off her shoulder? I've seen my mom's purse do that before when she's trying to hold my sister's hand."

Therapist:	"That is a great observation. You seem to think because her legs are straight and her purse has fallen off her shoulder that she might be working really hard to hold onto her daughter. I wonder what her daughter is doing that would force her mom to hold onto her arm that way?"
Client:	"Well, sometimes when my sister throws a fit in the store, my mom has to drag her out. I know that she sometimes seems embarrassed because everyone is looking. I hate it when my sister does that because everyone stares."
Therapist:	"You said some really important things. First, you noticed that they are out in public. That was good. Also, you talked about feeling embarrassed. Do you think the mom in this picture is feeling embarrassed?"
Client:	"I think she is. When I first saw the picture, I thought she was happy, but now, it looks like she's trying not to get mad and embarrassed because her daughter is throwing a fit. You can see some people around her, so I think they are out somewhere."
Therapist:	"I like how you noticed their surroundings. It is often important to remember where people are when considering their emotions as we often act differently in public than we would at home. I still wonder why the mom is smiling?"
Client:	"I think she is trying to keep it together because other people are looking. Maybe she is faking a smile to look like there's nothing

	wrong - like she's got everything under control. Her smile is way too big to be real."
Therapist:	"I like how you have inferred meaning behind her smile. It does seem awfully big and out of place. Sometimes, people may make a facial expression that is the opposite of their feelings. For example, laughing instead of crying, or smiling instead of frowning. Have you ever smiled like that mom in the picture when you weren't really happy?"
Client:	"One time I had to say the Pledge of Allegiance in front of my whole class and I was smiling so much that it made it hard for me to talk. I don't know why I did that, but I couldn't help it! I was really nervous and embarrassed because everyone was looking at me. Just like that mom in the picture. She probably wanted to run out of there, like I did that day in class."
Therapist:	"That's a great example! I really like how you are able to talk about your own feelings and compare them to the mom's in the picture. You are doing a nice job empathizing with the mom in that photo. I wanted to switch gears and have us make faces and use our body language to show different emotions. I am going to make a face like hers and I was hoping you'd stand in front of the mirror and try to copy me. Ready?"
Client:	"That's crazy. Why do we have to do that?"

Therapist: "Well, I have learned that it is much easier and faster to understand emotions and body language when we try it out for ourselves. Have you ever seen a toy in the store and thought it would be so much fun to play with, but it was stuck in the box and you couldn't play with it? That's kind of the way emotions are. Unless, we "take them out of the box" like the toy, we'll never know what it might be like to feel that way. Are you ready? It'll be fun, I promise."

Client: "Ok, I get it now. As long as it doesn't take forever and if it's too embarrassing, I'm not gonna do it!"

Therapist: "I appreciate you trying and if it makes you too uncomfortable, we can always stop and try something else, okay? First, I'm going to be the little kid and make some mad and sad faces. I want to see if you can copy mine."

NOTE: With older clients, more emotionally sophisticated clients, or upon completion of the initial modeling of this task, it might appropriate to go ahead to the next step and act out the social scenes being portrayed. Both the therapist and the client may choose a character from a social scene picture. They may act out the scene, or switch roles if desired. Initially, this may seem overwhelming to the client because it requires contrived emotional expression, but having the client "feel" the emotions being expressed will aid their ability to empathize with a variety of individuals and social roles throughout their world. In addition, acting out the social scene together allows for social context to be created for the emotions being displayed. It will be a memorable experience for the client and allow greater retention and understanding.

Step Three: Therapeutic Role Play

After modeling and practicing a few of the emotions portrayed in the photos, the therapist may wish to begin role-playing the social scenes portrayed in the photos.

This is the time to create levity within the therapy room by allowing silly and over-dramatized emotions and body language. The hope is to offer a safe environment for the client to "test out" new displays of emotion and become more aware of their own facial expressions and body language while displaying emotions. Positively reinforce their efforts and redirect any "misperceptions" that occur when the client interprets or displays new emotional situations.

Using terms "right" and "wrong" in response to a client's emotional displays may create anxiety and does not necessarily positively reinforce their efforts. Instead, regard their attempt at emotional portrayals with positive words and offer an alternative explanation for the emotion depicted if it falls short of the mark. For example, if a client misperceives an emotion depicted in a photo and proceeds to act out the wrong emotion. You might say, "I can really see where that person looks angry. You did a great job showing that. I wonder if maybe that person is also feeling sad? Let's look at the picture again to see." This type of "curious George" detective-like questioning fosters an atmosphere of acceptance and redirection without giving the child negative feedback.

A positive atmosphere and patience remain the keys for providing a healthy learning environment for the client to acquire skills without feeling shame or disapproval. I emphasize the need for an "open and caring" environment, as acting out emotions and social scenarios may feel embarrassing and create vulnerability for many individuals. Over time, clients will become accustomed to this type of emotional interchange.

The following is sample dialogue representing the same story as the dialogue in the previous section. However, this time, the client is older and the therapist will continue with some role-playing after the picture has been discussed. This next sample is also a good demonstration of an exchange that may take place for individuals with more sophisticated knowledge of emotional and social situations, regardless of chronological age.

Sample Dialogue: (Therapist and Adolescent Boy)

Therapist: "Ok, now that we've described some photos and built vocabulary, this would be a great time to practice your ability to name certain emotions by looking at photos. So, I would like for you to look at this photo and tell me what emotion you feel this lady is displaying."

Client: "Well, it looks like she's smiling, so maybe she's happy. But, she's also holding onto her daughter's hand really tightly, like maybe her daughter was in trouble. Her kid looks sad as she cries. Maybe the mom is mad, but trying to look like she's not with a big smile."

Therapist: "Wow! I really liked how you picked that out. Even though she's smiling, her smile looks really big and almost fake as her daughter is crying. I wonder what emotion might make her want to smile like that while her daughter is crying and carrying on?"

Client: "Well, it looks like other people are around, so maybe they're out in public. If my kid were crying like that, I'd feel really embarrassed. I don't know if I'd be smiling, or yelling, but I'd feel embarrassed because my kid was making such a big scene in public."

Therapist:	"You really hit the nail on the head. I agree that she's feeling embarrassed. It doesn't appear so, but her body shows us that she's stiff and tense. Also, she's got quite a grip on her daughter's hand like she's trying to pull her away from wherever they are. I think this would be a great time to role play this scenario. I want to play with this emotion a bit and try it out. Can you stand up with me and look in the mirror?"
Client:	"I think I will feel kind of funny doing this. Do we have to?"
Therapist:	"The best way to learn and improve upon our knowledge of emotions is to try them out in different ways. Looking in the mirror and at me will give your brain important messages about how to remember all of this information. It is also important to try and work with emotions to get better at identifying social situations quickly. I want you to feel these emotions in this photo for just a bit to understand this scenario. I'm going to pretend and be the little kid and I want you to be the mom and try and get me out of the store."
Client:	(standing in front of the full-length mirror) "That's kind of weird, but I think I understand what you are saying. "
Therapist:	"Great. Here we go – this is going to be fun, I love acting like the little kid. (Therapist taking a breath and getting into

the role of the child now). Mommy!!!!! I want some CANDY!!!!! I want it right now! Get me some CAAANNDYYY – Please?!? (crying, screaming, stomping feet, and making fists by her side) GET IT NOW!!!! MOMMY!!!!"

Client: (Watching the spectacle the therapist is creating with shock and horror.) "Oh my goodness! Don't scream! Stop that! Stop that right now, we're leaving!" (Getting a mad face).

Therapist: "NOOOOOO!!!!! MOMMEEEE!!!! If I don't get my candy, I'm gonna scream! AAGGHHHH!"

Client: (Starts looking around and getting a big grin on his face). "Ok, I feel this now. She's trying to get her out, but embarrassed that others are watching. Wow, I'm glad I don't have any kids yet."

Therapist: "You did a great job! So, we've also learned that even if we can feel the same emotion, our facial expression and body language may look different from person to person. Had you and I really been in a grocery store and I did this, you might have reacted differently. However, I think you felt a bit of the embarrassment that she might be feeling. Great job! Ready for kids yet?"

Client: (Laughing) "No, I think it'll be a while. That was kind of fun. Should we do another?"

Therapist: "We will do another soon. Right now, I think we'll switch gears and try something new."

Step Four: Practice, Practice, Practice!

After the initial steps have been taken to introduce and establish the task, this task should be incorporated any time a new emotion or social scene arises. For example, whilst in the midst of a session, if you realize that your client does not understand a particular emotion, or social scenario, make a note of it. Then, when appropriate, create a vocabulary card and use this task to practice the new learned emotions.

When practicing these various emotions and social scenarios, it will remain important to focus upon the client's visualization. Therefore, if the photo does not display the desired emotion, encourage the client to image a person displaying that emotion. The therapist may choose to model the facial expression and body language and ask the client to picture someone else using the same facial expression and body language. This will begin the ever-important visualization process discussed previously in the book and addressed in subsequent chapters regarding the retention of new social concepts.

The therapist is encouraged to use the language, "What do you see for a person who is happy, sad, jealous, etc…?" in order to boost their ability to image how a person might physically look when experiencing these emotions. The therapist may quiz the client and ask them to display a range of emotions using their facial expressions and body language for additional practice.

 Asking the client to verbalize throughout these exercises strengthens their ability to verbalize abstract concepts. By creating a link between their body movements and verbal expressions regarding those movements, the client will improve their imagery of emotional expressions. The ability to visualize will enable the client to retrieve and process emotional stimuli with greater speed and accuracy while maneuvering themselves throughout their social world.

The process of stimulating your clients' visualization will be described in greater detail in the following chapter.

Group and Family Format

Step One: Introduction and Finding Pictures

The therapist will introduce the task and begin to expose the group or family to a variety of social scenarios and emotions using photos, or magazines. Any obvious or presenting issues within the group or family members regarding social scenarios and emotions should be initially addressed. The therapist may also ask the group or family to choose a social scene from this book, or magazine from which to work.

In addition, emotional and social vocabulary should be built upon assuring that the group or family is capable of comprehending all emotions being discussed. The introductory time is vital for building rapport by encouraging a positive and comfortable environment open to emotional expression.

Step Two: Therapeutic Modeling

The therapist will begin to model emotions and social scenarios from the social scene chosen by the family or group. Various members of the family or group may be asked to mimic the facial expressions and body language while using the mirror for feedback. All group members may take turns modeling the same expression or model different emotions. The choice will depend upon the group dynamics, as well as age and abilities of the participants.

The therapist may ask one group member to show the rest of the group a facial expression for identification. One might turn this into a game entitled, "Guess that Emotion." An additional option would be the therapist showing the group a facial expression with inappropriate body language (body language not matching the given emotion) and then ask the group to correct the error by modeling the appropriate combination of facial expressions and body language. The goal for this process is to build exposure regarding the "look" of emotions and increase visual imagery using physical and visual feedback improving upon their recognition, mimicry, and comprehension of various emotions.

Step Three: Therapeutic Role Play

The therapist may role play the social scenarios depicted in the photos with the family or group establishing improved understanding of emotions. The therapist should ensure the group feels safe acting out particular roles within the social scenes. Role switching amongst group members should be encouraged allowing individuals the opportunity to play various roles within a social scenario. Emotions should be discussed as they arise during the course of role play exercises allowing deeper emotional processing.

Positive feedback regarding the member's portrayal of emotions remains vital to this process creating a safe environment fostering the group's learning. Any misconceptions or misinterpretations of emotional and social cues should be addressed by the therapist resulting in the strengthening of the group's abilities to interpret, comprehend, and execute new emotional behaviors.

Step Four: Practice, Practice, Practice!

The therapist and group may decide to practice a range of emotions and social scenarios within one session, or practice one social scenario and move forward with the remainder of the program. This task will continue to be an ongoing process over the course of treatment building new emotional and social vocabulary, as well as creating the opportunity to experience "emotions and social situations within a safe and comfortable environment.

Review of Facial Expression and Body Language Ste

1) **Step One: Introduction and Finding Pictures**

    - Therapist begins to expose the client to a variety of social scenarios and emotions using photos or magazines. Emotional and social vocabulary are developed assuring comprehension of emotions being discussed. A strong rapport is created encouraging emotional expression and a comfortable working environment.

2) **Step Two: Therapeutic Modeling**

    - Therapist begins to model various emotions and characters within the social scenes. Client asked to model these expressions using their face and body while looking in a mirror receiving physical and visual feedback. Emphasis placed upon the recognition and interpretation of facial expressions and body language associated with the emotions being discussed.

3) **Step Three: Therapeutic Role Play**

    - Therapist role plays social scenarios with the client creating greater understanding of emotions. Therapist and client enact various emotions developing a deeper comprehension of emotions under discussion.

    - Therapist continues to build positive rapport with client by offering positive feedback regarding the client's portrayal of emotions.

121

- Therapist may resolve any misconceptions, or misinterpretations of emotional and social cues client possesses. Through continual positive interchange, the client will continue to strengthen communication skills, interpretation, comprehension, and execution of new emotional behaviors.

3) **Step Four: Practice, practice, practice!**

    - Therapist and client practice a range of emotions and social scenarios as an ongoing process over the course of treatment.

Part Three:

Boosting the Mind's Eye

~11~
Building the Visual Abilities

Why Imagery?

Ian Robertson, a professor of psychology and director of the Institute of Neuroscience, discusses the importance imagery bestows upon language and one's overall life. In his book, *Opening the Mind's Eye*, he defines mental imagery as all of the bodily sensations one can recreate within one's mind - be it sights, smells, tastes, touch, and sounds. He asserts that Western society relies heavily upon language as the modus-operandi; therefore, people have inevitably lost a great deal of their visualization abilities because they are not utilized to the same extent as their verbal abilities.[1]

Children have vivid imaginations that appear to lose their vibrancy as they gain more education and language. Therefore, are words and verbal abilities literally stifling their ability to image? That might be one explanation. However, I often hear the opinion presented that video games, movies, and television have decreased children's ability to create mental images, as technology does much of the work for them. Regardless of why or how a person lacks imagery stimulation within their environment, I believe an individual's imaging abilities remain intact, but dormant, desiring practice and repetition to be revived from their sleeping state.

Robertson uses the adept skills of London taxi drivers to exemplify the significance imagery can have upon a person's daily functioning. He describes the taxi drivers' familiarity with the spatial layout of London to be so heightened they are capable of creating the shortest route from one point to another by accessing a map of the city within their mind's eye. Interestingly, when compared to their less experienced counterparts, highly experienced London taxi drivers have an enlarged hippocampus, or part of the brain involving emotions, navigation, and spatial orientation. The experienced taxi drivers' brains had adapted and created more efficient neural circuitry over time because of their daily visualization experiences.

This evidence reveals the malleability of the brain's functions, as well as the adaptability to improve upon one's visualization with greater practice and experience. As one visualizes more, their brain adjusts, adapts, and allows greater imagery abilities to take place.

The question begs: "Why is the ability to visualize important to me?" I would offer that visualization processes remain as vital to human functioning as the ability to verbalize with fluency. One buffers the other; therefore, if both are stimulated and adequately developed, our social and professional lives would experience greater fluidity. We would comprehend, process, memorize, write, and speak with greater competency if we tapped into the full breadth of our imaging abilities.

The mind has an awesome ability to categorize vast amounts of information. Language is one method that allows for the ability to classify enormous quantities of information being experienced, filtered, and processed every second of every day. However, language alone is not sufficient to process the daily sensory exposure bombarding our brains. Heightening visualization abilities will create greater proficiency within one's thinking processes.

Our Busy Lives

When you stop and ponder our busy modern lives and the awesome amount of stimulation we experience on a daily basis, the complexity alone is mind boggling. The noise, traffic, conversation, multi-tasking, computers, phones, blackberries, text messaging, driving, speaking, working, parenting, cooking, cleaning, hurrying, playing, etc. are but a few examples of the fullness of contemporary society. We have *so much* to attend to within a certain amount of time that we often go into "auto-pilot" throughout portions of our day proceeding through the motions of work and home.

How does this affect social and emotional exchanges? As Daniel Goleman discusses in his compelling book, *Social Intelligence*, we often treat one another as an "It" instead of a "You." In other words, we depersonalize many of our daily exchanges by treating others around us as merely an "it," or another "thing" that must be dealt with in order to move onto the next portion of our day.[2]

Before you feel offended at such a thought, *"I* am kind and *do not* treat others as 'Its!"*; I want you to close your eyes and recount your last visit to a fast-food drive-through. Imagine your rapid fire conversation with the ordering attendant through the microphone-sign, the efficiency with which your money is whisked away in exchange for change as bags of hot food are thrust out the window into your hurried hands. As you throw the bags and change aside, shove your car into drive knowing a line of 5 cars waits impatiently behind you, you may toss out a quick "thanks" with a half nod to the person inside of the window.

This is the social "It" exchange of which Goleman speaks. You and the fast-food attendant probably treated one another as "Its" in that situation. We all have treated others as "Its." The percentage may be higher or lower for every individual; however the point remains that we in some instance have treated another person as an entity rather than a person. I see this is an issue when we often treat the ones we love as "Its" in order to accomplish our daily routines and goals. I am not condoning the "It" treatment to fast-food workers either; however, I think our fast-paced lifestyle requires some form of depersonalization in order to continue at this pace. Or does it? Or more importantly, should it?

I feel we have allowed ourselves to become too focused upon the outcome within our experiences versus the process taken to accomplish that outcome. We have become an impatient, quick-rewards society demanding "more" faster and sooner. Hence, one may not cherish and value the steps encountered along the "road of life."

Because we hurry to succeed, improve, create, move, build, and make more, I wonder if our agendas have created a habit of not attending to the details around us (i.e. a person's face, body language, tone of voice, etc.). Before the invention of many of our technological advances, people relied upon relationships and social cues to maneuver through their daily tasks. They walked from here to there, looked others in the eye, spoke face-to-face, and wrote their thoughts down on paper (yes, actual paper and not on a keyboard!)

People in the past did not have the luxury of hiding inside of cars behind sunglasses and tinted windows racing past others traveling 75 miles per hour. Nor did they have e-mail, cell phones, and faxes to relay important information. They had to rely upon personal communication involving direct face-to-face contact. Maybe they were forced to watch and absorb more body language, facial expressions, eye movement, mouth movement, hand positions, posture, and tone of voice throughout the course of their day. I am not suggesting that they were necessarily "better" at these skills, but I wonder if they experienced the vast amount of inattentiveness, depression, and anxiety within their children and adults that modern society currently faces? Are these issues symptoms of our times, or merely diagnosed more often because they are recognized as symptoms?

I wonder if the de-emphasis in our modern society of personal, intimate exchanges remains one of the roots of a "social and emotional deficits" epidemic? We desire happiness and emotional stability, yet we often physically isolate ourselves behind computers, cell phones, and TVs for a large portion of our day. How can we teach our children to become more attentive, caring, and empathetic when we work longer hours and do not model these behaviors for them?

To exemplify our lack of overall attentiveness within our environment, a psychological experiment demonstrates a phenomenon called "change blindness." Individuals (the subjects of the experiment) were asked directions from a "stranger" (the experimenters). During their conversation, men carrying a door would pass between the speaking duo blocking the stranger with whom they were speaking, at which time the stranger was replaced by a completely different person. 50% of the people within the study *never noticed* that the stranger they were initially giving directions to was *not the same person* with whom they were speaking with after the door passed between them.[1]

This phenomenon called "change blindness" is based upon the idea of attention. We often attend so heavily to the instructions and the task itself that we no longer attend to the person with whom we are speaking. In essence, our brain has gone into automatic mode and is more focused upon the task than the person. This is Goleman's idea of treating others as an "It" versus the more humanistic "You".

In some situations, treating others as "Its" may prove to be efficient as it allows us to proceed throughout our day accomplishing numerous tasks. Not every conversation has to be a meaningful, "soul-wrenching" experience leaving us feeling warm and fuzzy. We do not necessarily have to discuss feelings that French fries elicit within us to the fast-food attendant in the drive-through line. On the other hand, we do not have to allow ourselves to function like heartless robots taking no notice of others around us. I believe we

should attempt to strike a balance between the effi
our "It" and the warmth of our "You" selves.

Personal Anecdote

One day, while waiting in line at Starbucks, I was being observed by an interested lady as I was giving an "empathy talk" to my 2 and 4 year old daughters. The 4-year old had undoubtedly snatched a treasured item from her sister – such is the life with siblings close in age – and the youngest bopped her sister on the head. I huddled my girls close together in a small group hug and squatted down until I was eye-level before launching into one of my "mini-talks" about the effects of their behavior. I asked my eldest how she would feel if her sister had taken away her toy. We talked about how hitting one another "makes things worse and hurts feelings." After a group hug, the understanding of how one's behavior can hurt another, and apologies all around, the observing lady commented on how nice it was that I had taken the time to explain to my girls the consequences of their behavior (not to mention my sigh of relief that all was well for the next 5 minutes).

My philosophy has always been "no time like the present" when dealing with my children; therefore, I would often have these moments wherever they occurred – grocery stores, restaurants, and friend's houses. This can be difficult and exerts quite a bit of mental and emotional energy, but is much more effective than getting upset and stomping around like an enraged and embarrassed parent.

I had not given a great deal of thought into my "public parenting" habits; yet, I realized that the observant lady's point was clear. She valued the direct teaching of emotional and social information because she felt that some parents did not take the time to directly teach their children these skills.

This story is not intended to gloat regarding my parenting techniques, or win the "Mother of the Year" award (although if presented with one, I would not turn it away). On the contrary, this story illustrates the numerous ways that we, as parents, must make an effort to directly educate our children with emotional and social information. Often the consistent "small" interactions (i.e. taking the time to explain and redirect behavior) help teach children the skills that will increase their ability to appropriately navigate their social worlds. As a society, we tend to focus upon teaching very young children reading, writing, and math skills assuming they will just "pick up" the social and emotional development necessary for successful functioning. As parents, educators, and professionals, we should take the time to directly teach children emotional and social skills beginning at birth.

In addition to direct stimulation of these skills, children must also learn through behavioral modeling. This implies that we must be more cognizant of our behaviors providing a positive role-model to our children. If we do not attend to the social and emotional cues within our surrounding environment, how can we expect our children to do so? How we choose to interact with our spouses, family, children, and co-workers directly impacts our children's behavior because they are close observers and take copious mental notes.

As a therapist, one of the more frustrating professional scenarios is when parents enter the office, point their finger at their child, rattle off diagnoses and how the child and everyone else is to blame for their behavior, and then ask you to "fix" the child (luckily, this does not occur very frequently). With a lot of deep breathing and patience on my part, I explain to the parents that this child's behavior does not occur in a vacuum; therefore, finger-pointing and "fixing" are not terms appropriate for helpful intervention. On the opposite end of that parental spectrum, I have witnessed parents blame themselves completely for their child's behaviors or diagnoses. This too is faulty thinking, as no one person is to blame (and blaming on the whole is counterproductive). Openness and flexibility in one's thoughts and behaviors are the keys allowing families and individuals to develop socially and emotionally. Through family education, parent skills training, individual intervention, and social and emotional skills development, many of the presenting issues are resolvable.

~12~
Imaging a Social Scene

Imaging for Life

One of the most vital components of this program remains the stimulation of one's imaging, or visualization abilities. As previously mentioned in regards to Dual Coding Theory (DCT), humans have the capacity to represent information both verbally and visually. Concrete concepts are more easily imaged because they retain physical characteristics tapping into our senses. Imaging abstract concepts becomes increasingly more difficult because abstraction lacks tangentiality - as 'abstract' means literally "to draw out" an idea from a concrete example.

Boosting the Mind's Eye attempts to reduce complex abstract concepts into smaller concrete bits of information by anchoring abstraction with concrete imagery. For example, photos, drawings, the therapist's enactment of emotions, therapeutic modeling, role-playing, mimicry, mirrors, vocabulary cards, etc. have all been incorporated to concretize abstract emotional and social concepts. By developing one's ability to image social situations, while simultaneously bolstering abstract vocabulary, a stronger foundation for the interpretation and comprehension of social information may emerge.

In addition to DCT and its emphasis upon the brain's

ability to encode information in order to learn and communicate, the question remains: How will the visualization portion of the program positively affect one's EI skills?

As mentioned previously, the Four-Branch model of EI offers a thorough analysis regarding the various components necessary for the development of social and emotional skills. The first section of this program, which focused upon building one's verbal abilities in regards to social and emotional language, allowed for the strengthening of an individual's perception of one's own and other's emotional states (Branch 1), as well as the ability to understand emotions based upon one's comprehension of emotional labels and categories (Branch 3).

More importantly, the first section of this program created steps to encourage the acquisition, understanding, and use of new emotional labels and social scenarios. However, in order for this information to be retained at the forefront of one's knowledge, the visual components of the brain must be further developed. One would not wish to work rigorously at acquiring knowledge only to repeat the necessary steps without making it a permanent part of their memory. Bombarding an individual with redundant and repetitive information beyond their comprehension accomplishes nothing more than feelings of frustration and failure.

The following section of the program intends to develop mental imagery in conjunction with the Four-Branch Model of EI, specifically tapping into *Branch 2: Using Emotions to Facilitate Thought* and *Branch 4: Managing Emotions*. As previously discussed, Branch 2 involves the employment and channeling of one's emotional state becoming a more effective decision maker and creative thinker. This idea rests in opposition to traditional views stating that cognition, or thought, drives emotion.[1] Instead, emotions give humans the ability to prioritize the cognitive system attending to the most crucial task at hand. In addition, emotions offer individuals an opportunity to use changes within their mood state to view situations from alternative perspectives.[2]

For example, the fight or flight response illustrates this concept. When faced with aversive stimuli, humans will often respond by either fighting or fleeing. One might consider an initial fear response to the stimuli as orchestrating a desire to run; however, if the person's fear were reduced by their recognition that the stimuli was not so aversive, they may no longer feel fearful and decide to remain in that particular environment. Or, maybe they were feeling particularly stressed that day and decided, "What the heck? I have nothing to lose" shifting their behavior from fleeing to fighting. Human emotion is quite powerful and creates adaptability and flexibility in both thoughts and behaviors. The challenge remains to become emotionally self-aware when utilizing emotion as an appropriate driving force behind thought and behavior versus being driven by one's emotions.

As this program continues to aid verbal and imaging abilities pertaining to social and emotional information, the final goal reflects the concepts based within *Branch 4 – Managing Emotions*. This includes the ability to process not only one's emotions, but also the emotions of others.[2] Clearly identifying and comprehending one's social and emotional environment enhances the ability to self-regulate, manage, and process not only personal emotions, but that of others. Self-regulation provides an individual with a fundamental skill boosting overall functioning within one's environment.

Duke et al. (1996) offer a step within their book, *Teaching Your Child the Language of Social Success*, they term "object-imaging." This includes a child looking at magazines and studying the nonverbal information within the picture in order to make an image within their mind's eye. Also, they discuss using videos and *in vivo* experience in order to solidify the recognition of emotional expression. The following step illustrated within *Boosting the Mind's Eye* expands that idea by focusing upon a person's imaging abilities throughout the process. The ultimate goal of this program focuses upon the development of a person's visualization skills providing a permanent foundation for the comprehension of emotional and social information.

The preceding program steps focused upon bolstering an individual's vocabulary, verbal expression, and exposure to concrete (photos) emotional information. These steps created the necessary stepping stones for an individual to verbalize an image within their mind's eye. Without sufficient language to express one's thoughts, emotions, images, etc., the ability to express images remains stunted.

Imaging exists as a principal cognitive process involved in language acquisition, retention, and comprehension. However, with the understanding of Dual Coding Theory, researchers have stipulated the necessity of the involvement of both verbal and imaging processes for language acquisition. Therefore, the idea that one should further stimulate imaging abilities does not appear far-fetched. As seen with the Visualizing and Verbalizing® program, Nanci Bell has shown that improving upon one's imaging abilities helps with the comprehension of reading material.[3] Hence, the application of imagery and verbal development to emotional intelligence seems to be a logical and valuable choice.

Suggestions for Sessions

You may find that pacing your sessions by spending shorter amounts of time on alternative tasks improves focus and minimizes frustration. Challenging your clients to improve their skills, while simultaneously fostering self-esteem and self-confidence, becomes a delicate dance between practitioner and client. Verbalizing your belief in their skills proves to be a powerful reinforcement by empowering their feelings of independence and autonomy. Often they begin to internalize your confidence in their abilities promoting independence and critical thinking skills.

When training professionals, I have often reiterated that one of the most powerful tools you possess is your ability to *take a one-down position* with your clients. Give your clients (mine are often children or adolescents) the opportunity to be "right" more often. Allow them to be an "expert" during their time with you, as they often feel "wrong" throughout their lives. One way to accomplish this task is to continually ask your clients questions throughout this process, instead of providing answers. This allows them an opportunity to think critically and realize they possess many answers to their own questions.

In my professional experience, individuals with language, comprehension, social, and emotional difficulties have learned to depend upon others for help, as they have been unable to act independently (or perceived they were unable to do so) – until now. Your clients will find within themselves a key to unlocking their hidden potential - a potential they have always possessed; but required direction to find. You hold the instructions for opening this gift, but it is your job to *allow them* to open this gift themselves. The independence you help to build will last a lifetime!

Step One: Creating a Sentence

In order to get started, choose a vocabulary term that has been previously worked and write it into an active sentence. For example, if the vocabulary term is "frustration," write this word into an active sentence that can be easily imagined. Such as, "The man showed his frustration at his daughter by kicking the leg of the table." Notice the sentence contains concrete content which allows for greater imaging ability compared to the following sentence, "The man heard frustration in his wife's voice." Although this sentence uses the term frustration, it does not clearly represent its meaning in a highly imaginable (and concrete) fashion.

Help develop images that are salient and easily pictured.

Humorous images, as well as personal examples befitting the vocabulary term are always helpful. If you feel the client is capable of creating their own sentence demonstrating active and concrete content, allow them to create the sentence. A client's personal examples will be the best possible usage of the term, as they can retrieve memories to aid imagery.

Step Two: Imaging and Fine Tuning

Initially, the sentence should be written by the therapist and read to the client. As time progresses, the client may write their own sentences and read them aloud. In the beginning; however, the therapist will write and read the sentence asking the client to focus solely upon creating an image in their mind's eye. If a client has a comorbid reading or comprehension issue, asking them to read and write might complicate the process and create unnecessary frustration. When reading the statement to your client, remember to read slowly and use appropriate intonation maximizing interest for the listener. Deliberate reading allows your client to create images with greater ease.

Ask the client to imagine the man in the previous example behaving in this fashion (the man kicking the table leg) and describe what they picture for this scene. The therapist's job is to question the client ascertaining enough information ensuring the client is truly picturing this sentence and not merely repeating the sentence back to the therapist.

Often individuals who have difficulty making mental images are very adept at remembering and repeating language. They have often survived through school by using a well-developed auditory memory permitting them to repeat large passages of language. Do not let this fool you! This does not mean that they are imaging, or comprehending, but are merely mimicking what they have heard. Mimicry (or shallow recall) is often a coping mechanism offering short-term success throughout their academic environment.

Evoke sufficient detail from the client ensuring imagery is taking place. The details may concern the physical look of the man, his facial expressions, body language, sound of his voice, background to the scene, and other important characters in the sentence. I ask my clients to "make a movie in their head" to exemplify the visualization process. I remind them that movies contain a beginning, middle, and end. Therefore, would a movie be easily understood if someone only saw the middle portion of it? Hence, their description of their movie should be sequential and organized giving life to their image.

Recognize and accept that many individuals may not be able to visualize a "movie" playing in their head – just yet. They see only bits and pieces of imagery, or nothing at all. Do not be alarmed by this. In order for them to learn to create mental images, they will have to build this process over time with repetition and consistent stimulation.

Initially, the details of the sentence will be retrieved by the therapist's questioning technique, as the client may not be able to verbalize or image with relative ease. In order to essentially create an image for the client, the therapist should use choice/contrast questioning. Only a couple of choices are offered at one time, so as not to overwhelm the client's capacity for imagery. For example, "Is the man tall or short? Fat or thin? Frowning or smiling?" Remember, the focus is upon the emotional and social content of the image. Therefore, do not focus upon nit-picky details beyond the necessary physical descriptors. The focus should remain upon facial expressions, body language, tone of voice, social context, posture, mood, perspective, etc.

Step Three: Critical Thinking Skills

Use follow-up questions throughout the imaging process evoking critical thinking regarding the occurrence of the social scenario. Some example questions might be: "Why does that person show that particular facial expression? What do you think will happen next? Have you ever felt that way? I wonder what you would do in that situation? I wonder what led up to this social scenario? Will anyone else be affected by this person's behavior and in what way?"

If the therapist allows sufficient repetition and stimulation of imagery development, this process will improve each successive session. You may find your client's imaging abilities developing slowly and steadily, or simply "switching on" one day like a light switch. These differences are as individual as the neural networks in the human brain; however, improvement will eventually occur as the client is continually stimulated to access the visual processes within the brain.

NOTE: Remember to pace your session according to your client's capabilities. If you client is able to create vivid images within their mind's eye, this step should be completed in one or two attempts, and then progress onto imaging whole stories. However, if your client retains difficulty when making mental images, remain with this step and slowly build imagery throughout subsequent sessions. The goal remains to build upon emotional knowledge; therefore, one should never aspire to create the "perfect" mental image. The big picture of this entire process is merely to further develop visualization bolstering comprehension of social and emotional information.

Sample Dialogue: (Therapist and 12 Year-Old Boy)

Therapist:	"I have a sentence I want to read to you so you can make a movie in your head. I will read the sentence and I want you to try and make a picture in your head so we can talk about what you see. You ready? The sentence is: 'The man showed his frustration at his daughter by kicking the leg of the table.' Can

	you tell me what you see for that?"
Client:	"I see a man who is frustrated with his daughter kicking the leg of a table."
Therapist:	"You were able to tell me the words and that's a good start. Can you tell me how old you picture these characters to be?"
Client:	"A younger dad, maybe in his 30's and a 5-year-old girl."
Therapist:	"Great. Can you tell me a little more about what they look like in your image?"
Client:	"The man has brown hair and the girl looks just like her dad. They both look really mad."
Therapist:	"Ok, I'm starting to see this scene. Can you tell me more about what you mean by 'looking like her dad?'"
Client:	"Well, they both have brown hair and I see them looking like my dad and little sister, who look alike in the face."
Therapist:	"That is a great comparison. I like how you're seeing your own family. I'm hearing you say that the dad and daughter in this story may share facial features, like their noses, eyes, and mouths are maybe similar?"
Client:	"Yeah, that's what I mean. My sister and dad have the same nose, brown eyes, and lips. I was seeing this girl and dad to actually look like my sister and dad."

Therapist:	"That is great. Where do you see this scene taking place?"
Client:	"I saw them inside our living room and the dad kicking the leg of our coffee table."
Therapist:	"So, you pictured your own living room. That's a good idea because it is easier to imagine something familiar. Can you tell me more detail about the room, so that I can picture what you picture?"
Client:	"Well, our living room has a red couch and a brown coffee table with a glass top. If anyone ever kicked it, they would probably break their toe!"
Therapist:	"I bet you are right. Did you see any particular look on his face, or facial expression, as the dad kicks the table leg?"
Client:	"He's frowning and I can hear him grumbling too… His hands are in fists by his side."
Therapist:	"Wow! I can really see that too. He sure doesn't look very happy. What about the little girl – do you image a facial expression for her?"
Client:	"I see her looking sad a little surprised that her dad kicked the leg of the table."
Therapist:	"What type of face might she have for those feelings?"
Client:	"Well…it's kind of hard to put into words."

Therapist:	"Sometimes it is hard to describe the looks people have on their faces. Can you show me with your face what you're picturing the girl's to look like? Then, we can put some words to it."
Client:	"Well, I saw her doing this... (sticking his lip out and then raising his eyebrows up and opening his mouth wide)."
Therapist:	"Wow...that was really good. Can you tell me with your words what type of faces you were making?"
Client:	"I was pouting first because the dad was yelling at me, then I looked surprised because he kicked the table leg."
Therapist:	"You did a really nice job illustrating how she might look. You said that she was pouting because she was being yelled at? What do you think might have led up to the dad kicking the table?"
Client:	"Maybe he got into a fight with someone. Or, got mad when he was at work."
Therapist:	"That's some good thinking. Let's reread the sentence and see if it tells us more. It states: *The man showed his frustration at his daughter by kicking the leg of the table.* Hearing that again, do you think he could've gotten mad at work, or that he was somehow upset with his daughter?"
Client:	"Oh! It said that he was frustrated with his daughter, so they probably got into some

	kind of argument."
Therapist:	"I wonder what type of disagreement might have occurred that the dad would react this way? Any thoughts?"
Client:	"Well, I know with our dad that he only gets really angry if we break things we're not supposed to. So, I pictured the little girl breaking her mom's favorite flower vase and the dad getting mad because it was all over the floor."
Therapist:	"That is a great example. I think it is interesting that the dad chose to kick the leg of the table if he didn't want things broken in the house. Do you think that his behavior was appropriate in that situation?"
Client:	"Not really. I think that if you don't want others to act like that then you should try not and act like that yourself."
Therapist:	"Good thinking. Do you think it's possible that something else happened throughout his day that contributed to his reaction to his daughter?"
Client:	"Yeah. Like I said, maybe he had a bad day at work or something."
Therapist:	"That could be very true. What other types of feelings do you think he might have besides frustration in this example?"
Client:	"Maybe angry and sad."

Therapist:	"I agree. If you were really frustrated about something, how would you show it with your face and body? What types of things would you do?"
Client:	"I would yell at someone, or throw my toys."
Therapist:	"Those behaviors would definitely show your anger. Let's talk about some different ways we might express our frustrations without necessarily harming our things, or other people's feelings."

As your client remains engaged and is prompted to imagine these social sentences, other questions or topics may arise. Take advantage of these conversations to discover new emotions and social situations requiring exploration. There is never a better time to educate than the present! These moments may be scarce during the very early sessions, as clients are building their abilities to image and verbalize their thoughts.

As your relationship with your client becomes more comfortable and their verbal expression increases, they may ask more in-depth questions. Be mindful of their curiosity and new found expressive abilities. This is a wonderful moment, so run with it and try not to get "bogged down" with the program steps. Instead, use this time to stop and engage them in conversation, while teaching them appropriate responses and behaviors. Your interaction with them may be more educational and therapeutic than program steps if aptly timed.

You may realize when this step becomes obsolete as their ability to visualize becomes stronger. As they build new concepts during vocabulary acquisition, they will often put these concepts into action spontaneously. When they begin to make these connections independently, this single sentence step will no longer be necessary.

Group and Family Format

Step One: Creating a Sentence

Write a sentence for the family or group using a previously completed vocabulary term. Be sure to use concrete ideas when writing the sentence making it easier to image. Engage the family or group to choose the vocabulary terms and create the sentence with you.

Step Two: Imaging and Fine Tuning

Read the sentence to the family or group and use the "Round Robin" technique to build an image. Start with one person in the group verbalizing a portion of the sentence. Go around the room and allow each person to add a piece of the picture so that the entire group has created an image. You may also ask one person within the family or group to create the image and allow others add to the image as needed.

There are many possibilities for group involvement, as creating images is a flexible and fun task. As the therapist, be sure to ask choice and contrast questions to fine-tune the image. Ask questions that will allow the group or family to image the facial expressions and body language of the characters within the sentence. You may decide to ask others in the group to question and clarify another individual's imagery promoting greater group involvement.

Step Three: Critical Thinking Skills

Once the image has been created and seems complete, begin to ask the family or group critical thinking skills questions pertaining to the social scene depicted. Some sample questions might be: "Why did the character(s) behave in that fashion? What types of feelings might they have been experiencing? Would you have behaved or felt that way if you were that character? Can you think of a time when you felt that way?"

There are no limits to this type of questioning. You may

decide to follow the group's lead when asking critical thinking skills questions. However, remember that this task can often derail in a group, as everyone may want to add in personal anecdotes. You may have to move forward and remind group members that additional time will be allotted for sharing their thoughts and feelings throughout the session.

Review of Imaging a Social Scene Steps

1) **Step One: Creating a Sentence**

    - Write an active sentence using a previously worked vocabulary term. Be sure to use concrete language easily imaged.

2) **Step Two: Imaging and Fine Tuning**

    - Read the sentence and ask them to verbalize their mental image. Use choice and contrast questioning fine tuning their mental image.
    - Ask questions pertaining to the imagery of facial expressions, body language, and pertinent social and emotional content within the sentence.

3) **Step Three: Critical Thinking Skills**

    - Ask critical thinking skills questions pertaining to the social and emotional content of the sentence. Why did that character feel, behave, react, etc. in that situation? How might the client have behaved or felt in that same situation?

~13~
Imaging Social Stories and Role Play

Once a client has developed their imaging ability beyond a single sentence, you may wish to introduce social stories. These scenarios are found in Appendix 4, or may be written by the therapist addressing pertinent therapeutic issues specific to the client's needs. A child's parents (or the child themselves) will discuss social situations evident as appropriate fodder from whence to work. This is a valuable opportunity for the therapist to utilize recent events in the child's life "driving home" social and emotional concepts.

When reading the social story, it may be necessary to read the passage to the client, or have them read it aloud – dependent upon the individual's reading capabilities. The focus of this task is to build visual imagery for the given scenario; therefore, all other mediating variables should be minimized to reduce frustration and anxiety.

Step 1: Reading, Imaging, and Exploring the Story

After reading the complete scenario aloud to the client (or have them read the passage aloud if appropriate), allow them to respond to the passage with thoughts or feelings about the scenario or characters within the story. You may specifically question their perceptions regarding a particular character's behavior within the social scenario.

"I wonder why..." statements engage individuals in this type of "investigative" detective work regarding emotional and social perception. For example, "I wonder why that lady laughed when he said that?" or "I wonder why that boy was frowning when his mother walked away?" These statements offer the client an introduction to discuss the emotional and social issues associated with the story. Socratic questioning allows the client the opportunity to think independently by "owning" their thoughts and feelings regarding the scenario being discussed.

After verbalizing their initial reaction to the social story, discuss anything that appears "socially strange" in the scenario allowing for the opportunity to discuss appropriate versus inappropriate behaviors within a given social situation.

As you discuss the social scenario, pay close attention to your client's level of comprehension pertaining to social and emotional vocabulary, as they may not understand all of the terms within a story. Create a running list of vocabulary words (to be visualized later in the session) ensuring that gaps of knowledge are filled. If the lack of comprehension is vast enough to inhibit inferred meaning from the story, you may pause the story creating vocabulary cards at that moment. Or, you may decide not to stop the story and briefly discuss the vocabulary term and create vocabulary cards later. Using your discretion will be vital in maintaining flow and rapport throughout the session.

Taking time to discuss new concepts in context offers the client an ability to understand social information as it may naturally appear within a social situation. It is important to be timely when discussing new vocabulary terms arising in the social story forming a stronger connection between the new words and the social context in which they appeared.

Once all of the concepts are explained and understood, read the passage a second time (if necessary to process the contents of the story). Use choice and contrast questioning as necessary to stimulate their imaging ability. You will find an individual's ability to comprehend a story remains contingent upon the speed and aptitude when making mental images. An individual with more advanced imagery abilities will process the social stories with greater efficiency and accuracy than those with spotty visualization development.

Regardless of whether or not an individual creates mental images matching the story, you will need to question abstract information or social subtleties within the passage. Often these concepts are difficult for individuals with social deficits to comprehend because they are not readily visualized. Your job will be to aid their visualization process by breaking down abstract concepts into smaller concrete ideas (concretizing). Use your language to guide their imagery.

Sample Dialogue: *(Therapist and Young Girl)*

> Therapist: "I am going to read a story to you and I want you to listen and try and make a movie in your head. I want you to try and see the characters in the story. Ready?" (The therapist then reads the following passage aloud.)

Family's Stressful Day
(Story found in Appendix 4)

It was a hot July day, and today was moving day. The whole family had their share of work to do. Billy, the big brother, had to move many boxes into the truck. Sally, the little sister, was supposed to vacuum the carpets as the rooms were emptied. Mom and Dad were moving furniture and boxes. Everyone was tired and grumpy.

Sally accidentally ran into Billy while she was vacuuming and he dropped a box with picture frames inside. CRASH!!!! The glass inside the box shattered. Billy was so angry that his face turned red and he balled up his fists and yelled, "SALLY! How could you do this? Now, all of Mom and Dad's pictures are ruined and it's all your fault! You are going to be in so much trouble!" Sally cried, "I'm sorry, Billy. I didn't see you, it was an accident. Please don't tell Mom and Dad that it was all MY fault!"

Billy stomped off to tattle to Mom and Dad. Mom and Dad walked into the room and saw that Sally had been crying. Dad put his arms around her and said, "It's ok Sally. We know it was an accident. Let's try and be more careful." Mom turned to Billy and stated, "Billy, you need to learn to control your temper. It is not nice to yell at your sister. You really hurt her feelings. I believe you owe her an apology."

Billy looked at his sister and quickly said, "I'm sorry." Dad said to everyone, "The important thing is that we all get along. Although we are tired and grouchy from the hard work, it does not give us the right to take it out on each other. Why don't we take a break and go get some ice cream? I think we all deserve a little treat."

Therapist:	"What are your thoughts about that story?"
Client:	"Well, I thought that Billy was being mean to his sister."
Therapist:	"He seemed pretty angry with her. Do you feel that he should have responded to her in that way?"
Client:	"I think he got too mad about it and was a tattle-tale."
Therapist:	"Yes, he did tell on her to their parents. I wonder why?"
Client:	"I know that sometimes I tattle on my brother because I don't want to get into trouble. If I

tattle on him, then my parents know that it is his fault and not mine."

Therapist: "That is a very good observation. I think it's good you know the reasons why you do certain things. Billy probably didn't want to get into trouble with his parents. Do you think he could have gone about that in a different way?"

Client: "Well, he could have been nicer about the whole thing."

Therapist: "I agree with you. Can you tell me a bit about what you were picturing for this story? You gave me some really nice answers about their behavior, but I'm interested in the movie you made in your head."

Client: "Well, I saw Billy yelling at Sally. I saw the parents talking to them."

Therapist: "Good. Can you tell me what you pictured for the kids? Were they younger or older?"

Client: "I saw Billy to be about 12 and Sally about 10 years old."

Therapist: "Okay - do you have any details pictured about Billy, Sally, or their parents you can share with me?"

Client: "Well, I saw Billy to be tall with brown hair. He was walking really fast with a big box of pictures. I think Sally might be blonde and smaller. I saw her run into him because she was busy doing something and didn't see

	him. I saw him get really mad and yell at her and she started to cry. Then, I saw the parents come in and the dad hug Sally."
Therapist:	"It sounds like you made a good movie in your head of this story. Earlier you told me your thoughts about the characters in this story and I would also like to hear how you feel about them. Would you have acted like any of the characters in that situation?"
Client:	"Well, I think Billy is mean for yelling at his sister. Sally didn't do it on purpose and he blamed everything on her. I think the Mom and Dad should have gotten angrier at Billy because he made Sally cry."
Therapist:	"I wonder why Billy was so angry?"
Client:	"I don't know! Maybe because he didn't like his sister and she got in his way."
Therapist:	"I think this story shows an important example that sometimes when we are frustrated, or tired, we can take our feelings out on other people. Do you think this might be true of Billy?"
Client:	"Well, I guess so. But, I still don't think that he should have been so mean to Sally."
Therapist:	"You're right. Just because we are tired, it doesn't mean we should take it out on others. What images did you make for Billy's body language and facial expressions that might have shown his mood?"

Client: "I saw him frowning and walking really slow like he was tired."

Therapist: "That's really good! Also, the story told us that his face got really red and he balled his hands into fists. This would also show that he is feeling anger. Can you imagine Billy with a really red face and fists made like this?" (Therapist demonstrates the facial expression and body language.)

Client: "I see that now. I didn't imagine him looking like that before. No wonder Sally cried. He looks really mad!"

Therapist: "Can you think of anything else Sally could have told Billy to help him understand her feelings?"

Client: "She could have told him not to yell at her and that it was an accident. She seemed really worried about her parents getting mad at her when Billy went to tattle on her."

Therapist: "That's very good. Yes, in the story she does tell him it's an accident and not to tattle on her. So, she did seem worried about him tattling on her. But, you're right; she could have asked him not to yell at her. She might have said that 'Yelling hurts her feelings and could he please calm down?' Also, can you think of why she might have been worried about Billy telling on her?"

Client: "Because she didn't want to get into trouble?"

Therapist:	"Besides getting into trouble, can you think of another feeling word that may have described how she felt?"
Client:	"Scared?"
Therapist:	"That is one feeling word. I am thinking of a word that tells how Sally may feel if her parents were not satisfied with her behavior. Can you think of that word?"
Client:	"No, I don't think so."
Therapist:	"The word I was looking for is disappointed. Sometimes when someone isn't happy with our behavior, they feel let down. Sally might have been worried that her parents would be disappointed in her because she broke the picture frames. Can you think of a time you might have felt that way?"
Client:	"One time I know I disappointed my parents because I hit my little sister. They looked really sad when I did that."
Therapist:	"Good job! Let's write this word down on a card so we remember to make a vocabulary word out of it later."
Client:	"I wanted to ask you one question. What did the mom mean when she told Billy to control his temper? I've heard my mom say that before, but I didn't know what she meant."
Therapist:	"That is a very good question! (Answering the question as she writes down the word 'temper' on a vocabulary card for later) What

the mom was trying to tell Billy was that he should try not to yell and get so upset. She wanted him to learn and stay calm the next time an accident happened, so as not to hurt anyone's feelings by yelling and screaming at them. Does that make sense to you?"

Client: "Oh yes, now it does."

Therapist: "Good. Now that we've read the story and talked about the feelings, let's pick some characters to play. It will be like a little play that we put on together. Which character in the story would you like to be?"

This step is complete once the client appears to comprehend and image the story, along with the characters and their emotions. Feel free to move forward, even if the client has not "perfected" the story. In other words, do not worry if every single concept or character is not imaged completely. You will have many opportunities and future stories to stimulate imagery. The focus should center upon a steady flow within the session while promoting a positive atmosphere of learning and fun (individuals often learn better while having fun – especially children!)

Step Two: Role Play

Once the story has been explored and imaged, it is time to do a little acting. This step may be quite enjoyable for both parties, as the client is able to re-enact social scenes in a comfortable setting. Even if the client is not overly dramatic, or is timid, this will be great practice for possible future social scenarios. Most individuals when asked to role-play for the first time are intimidated by this task. If you have not experienced a bit of theatrical drama, or role-play, you may feel a bit awkward as well. This is perfectly normal, as "stage fright" is a common experience amongst many individuals. This task is not intended to create the next generation of movie stars; but to promote experiential knowledge, stimulate imagery, and buffer one's empathy. Donning various roles (even if acting) promotes understanding of another's perspective.

Learning to verbalize and express oneself in a variety of social situations prepares an individual for the future. Even if that *exact* social scenario never occurs, your client will learn and experience bits and pieces of social knowledge seeping into their reservoir of emotional experience recallable for a future encounter. In addition, this step will strengthen your relationship with your client, as they learn to trust and interact with you when depicting various emotions.

Remember that all of these tasks encourage visualization of emotions and social scenarios boosting an individual's ability to retain and apply information in the future. By simultaneously stimulating imagery and verbalization, social and emotional information will be dually encoded facilitating the comprehension and efficiency of these processes by creating a deeper level of understanding.

When initiating this task, ask the client to enact a character in the story closely matching their personal characteristics (i.e. sex, age, role within a family, etc.). For example, if you have a young female client, let them play the young girl or young boy within the story. Try and delay your client playing an adult role until after they have witnessed your enactment of that role. This allows you the opportunity to model appropriate adult behavior for the subsequent role-reversal task.

As you portray the adult characters within the story, you will be modeling mature and socially appropriate responses to others' behavior. However, when you switch roles and play the child, it is a good idea to really "play it up" and "act out" giving the child an opportunity to witness and understand the difficulties parents (or other caregivers) experience when children display strong emotions. This will be discussed in greater detail in the next section.

When first attempting this task, choose an emotionally tempered scene to reduce the intimidation factor of emotional expression. This entire process may prove embarrassing and difficult for your client because you are requesting emotional openness and vulnerability. However, if *you express comfort and calmness* while displaying your own emotions, then you will model this behavior for your client. This task should be fun and approached with humor, which will decrease the pressure your client feels to "act" in a dramatic and contrived fashion. The more freedom you allow your client when displaying emotions and "getting into character," the wider array of emotions you will witness.

Sample Dialogue: (Therapist and Young Boy)
The roles are chosen from the scenario in the previous section.

Therapist:	"Now that we've discussed the story and understand all of the words and emotions in the story, I think it would be fun to role-play a bit. So, I want to have you act as Billy and I'll be the Mom. We will re-enact the story the way it was written, but I want us both to feel free to add in our own thoughts and feelings where we want to. Okay? There's really no right or wrong – I want us to have a bit of fun with this."
Client:	"This seems kinda weird. I'll feel stupid acting. I don't like that kind of thing."
Therapist:	"I know what you mean. It can sometimes be embarrassing to act in front of others. I think once we try a little, it might be fun. There are no lines to learn, so you can't mess anything up. Let's just give it a shot and see?"

Client:	"I guess, but if it's too dumb, I'm not doing it."
Therapist:	"Fair enough. Let's get started. You're Billy and I'm Mom, so I'm going to start lecturing you about yelling at Sally, okay?"
Client:	"Okay." (*smiling*)
Therapist:	"Billy – I don't understand why you are yelling and getting so upset at Sally. She said it was an accident. Why are you so angry?"
Client:	"I don't know. She should've been watching where she was going."
Therapist:	"Even though she should have been more careful, does it make it okay to yell at her when she makes a mistake?"
Client:	"It's not my fault - she is ALWAYS in the way!"
Therapist:	"Billy, no one was blaming you or your sister for breaking the picture frames. These things just happen sometimes, it was an *accident*."
Client:	"Yeah, but I always get in trouble whenever something bad happens."
Therapist:	"It is harder to be the older brother because we expect more from you. You have more responsibilities than your sister. But, how would you feel if Sally yelled and blamed you, then tattled about it to us?"

Client:	"Bad, I guess. I just didn't want to get into trouble. I wanted you to know that it was her fault, not mine."
Therapist:	"I understand how you feel. No one wants to get into trouble. It is important to think about how other people might feel before we act. That way, we might make better choices with our behavior. I want you to know that Dad and I love you both and know you will make mistakes sometimes. We all do and it's perfectly OKAY."
Client:	"Yeah, I guess so. I didn't think about that."
Therapist:	"Billy, we just want you to understand that accidents happen and we will be more upset if you hurt your sister's feelings than if you break something. Does that make sense?"
Client:	"Yes. I just didn't want you to be mad at me. I didn't know that I would make Sally cry."
Therapist:	"What do you think would be a good way to make up to Sally?"
Client:	"I guess I should tell her I'm sorry and I won't yell at her anymore?"
Therapist:	"I think that would be a great idea. I am proud of you for realizing how you might change your behavior in the future. You sure are growing up!"

As your client's age and gender will undoubtedly differ, you may choose different characters to portray as needed. In addition, this dialogue is geared towards a younger child.

You will find yourself shifting your speaking style when addressing older clients.

Step Three: Role-Reversal

Role playing is an effective technique lending first-hand experience when attempting novel methods of verbalizing emotions and socially appropriate responses. Role-reversal offers an even superior experiential opportunity than simply role playing by allowing one to safely switch social hats. This step fosters the client's understanding of various roles people experience in a myriad of social situations. By enacting diverse social roles, individuals will have the opportunity to experience the world as another might; thereby introducing the concept of *empathy*.

Empathy for All

What is empathy and why is it a vital component of social understanding? *Empathy* can be defined as the ***identification*** of another's feelings. The terms sympathy and empathy are often viewed as synonymous; however, a minor distinction exists. *Sympathy* is the *feeling of compassion* and pity one may feel for another, while empathy involves the ability to actually identify or "walk a mile in a person's shoes." Why is this distinction worth noting? Merely being able to sympathize with individuals, or feel compassion regarding their plight, is certainly a valid human emotion. However, if individuals are to mature emotionally, the ability to actually "feel" what another feels, or apply their own emotional knowledge and experiences to the feelings of another requires a deeper level of emotional understanding.

Empathy requires perspective-taking – a complicated concept for individuals primarily concrete in thought to comprehend. The ability to empathize involves flexibility in thought and emotion not occurring naturally for individuals with a rigid thought process. Regardless of one's position or stage in life, empathy is applicable to all. To exemplify this, imagine a corporate business offering training seminars to their employees designed to increase empathy fostering communication and a positive working environment. Employees might be asked to enact various roles within that particular business providing them an opportunity to experience the trials and tribulations of various business roles. Employees may find themselves more understanding and patient in future business situations because they have *personally* experienced the reality of another in an alternate role from their own.

How might it feel to be the boss, secretary, janitor, fast-food worker, middle manager, CEO, mail room worker, human resources worker, etc.? Through the "eyes of another," one may gain a broader perspective and thereby, treat others with greater respect and courtesy. Respectful and courteous behaviors are positive values worth teaching children of all ages, as human kindness remains a cornerstone pivotal to a positive future.

Empathy for Children

Empathy is not a skill appropriate solely for adults. Children, if taught to do so, can elicit empathetic feelings very early in life. Developmentally however, children cannot comprehend the vast and complex emotional world of adults and should not be held to this standard. I often remind parents that children are capable of grasping emotional language based upon their developmental age, not upon the desires and expectations their parents uphold. A 10 year-old child should learn to empathize and process emotional information appropriate to a 10 year-old child, not that of an adult who has a chronological advantage.

Because most children lack the quantity and quality of life experiences adults possess; they will not fully comprehend complex emotions tied to adult issues (i.e. stress associated with paying bills, feelings associated with divorce, fatigue associated with juggling work, home, etc.) Children often experience similar emotions to that of adults;

but on a more convoluted scale. This does not insinuate children's emotional experiences are lesser than that of adults - merely the content of the material they experience may be less intricate and complex compared to that of an adult. As a parent or professional, it is vital to remember not to diminish a child's experiences and feelings because the issue seems trivial comparable to adults. What we as adults deem trivial may be of the utmost importance to a child.

For example, a young child may not have experienced a painful romantic separation, but they have most likely felt the rejection of losing a friend on the playground. Their rejection and social shame is as valid as the rejection felt when adult romantic partners part ways. As adults, it is important to remember that even though "adult problems" seem bigger to us, children do not comprehend anything more than their limited world. Therefore, rejection, sadness, loss, embarrassment, etc. are just as crushing to them (if not more so because this may the first time they have experienced that particular emotion) as to an adult.

A wide range of emotions are imperative for children to experience in order to learn strategies for managing emotional turbulence throughout life. If their "less than pleasant" emotions are minimized by adults in the attempt to reduce discomfort or pain for the child, they will not learn effective coping strategies.

It is a good rule of thumb to listen to their stories and find the underlying issue or emotion being experienced. It may be difficult to extract a great deal of information or meaning from a recounted story, as children with language issues often do not verbalize in a sequential and fluent manner; however, the "real story" involving their feelings resides within their tangle of words. Help them rephrase, organize, and sequence their story developing their verbal abilities while stimulating their emotional expression.

Reflectively listening, summarizing, and restating their experiences in a logical and succinct fashion models your desired verbalization style. After a period of time, you might find they mimic this more efficient style of speaking when recounting their experiences. With the continual support and skills learned throughout this program (and with your patience and kind interaction), you will witness improvement in both their speaking and imaging abilities.

When Feeling Sad, Bad, & Mad is Ok!

Have you ever heard the expression, "Welcome to my world..."? I find myself becoming mildly irritated with this expression when I am recounting a particularly stressful day and merely needing someone to empathize with my feelings. I may be emotionally purging my soul to another to feel reassurance, support, or just to vent my emotions only to hear the listener smugly state, "Well, welcome to my world!"

Did they not hear a word of my experiences and feelings? Does that statement mean they've been experiencing this exact issue for quite some time and I've just now managed to catch up with *their* reality? Or, is it that *they too desire empathy* and are attempting to verbalize their empathy to me by stating that they understand my world because they've experienced it? It is usually the latter; however, I have often found that the tone of their statement is usually what spawns my frustration.

What happened to, "Wow - that sounds stressful!" Or, "Gee, I'm really sorry to hear that." This goes back to Therapy 101. When someone is feeling sad, crying, or depressed, their emotions can be diminished when someone says, "Don't be sad. Don't cry. It'll be okay. It's not that bad." Words used in the attempt to console can often negate a person's sense of self-awareness. In their mind, they may be thinking, "No, it's not alright! That's why I'm crying! Can't you see that I'm hurting? I want someone who can understand my pain and tell me its okay to feel this way."

But, if you've never had therapeutic training, how are you supposed to know that? Why shouldn't an individual cry and vent their emotions? Why can't an individual feel sad and downtrodden every now and again? Contrary to what Disney movies would have you believe, life is not one long theme park adventure filled with purely fantastical experiences. Life can be difficult, stressful, confusing, and sad and individuals need to understand one another's plight in life offering support when they are needed. Most of us desire to help another to feel "better." However, how does one offer genuine empathy without years of education in counseling?

I harp upon this point because I witness many children lacking in any conception of another's reality. As our society continues to stimulate and uphold a child's cognitive development, I feel we shelter them from certain emotional realities in life. I previously stated that children cannot fully empathize with adult issues and emotions; however, they can certainly be appropriately exposed to reality in a fashion preparing them for life's road blocks.

I digress with a personal story. My eldest daughter at the age of 5 taught me a valuable lesson regarding empathy as seen through the eyes of a child. One night while completing our lengthy bedtime ritual, she was expressing her feelings regarding a situation at school and began to recount her day (very slowly and in great detail). It was past her bedtime and I was impatiently listening to her story because I recognized her stalling behavior (a patterned routine since age 2). Although my language feigned interest in her school drama, my facial expressions and body language must have betrayed me because she stopped her story, looked at me with exasperation and exclaimed, "MOM! How am I supposed to feel when you don't even let me finish what I'm saying? I don't think you really care about my day and just want me to hurry up and go to bed!"

Remembering that she is the daughter of a therapist and often uses my psychological warfare against me, I will state that her comment was profound. I was minimizing her social experience with my impatience and desire for her to quickly verbalize her story. She recognized the lack of interest in my tone and called me on it. It was great! However, at that moment, I realized that my tone of voice, body language, and facial expression undermined my words. She perceived my impatience because my body and face deceived my verbalizations. This led me to understand why I interpreted the "Well, welcome to my world" comment to be one of sarcasm and smugness dependent upon the *tone* used by the speaker. My daughter and I experienced a mini role-reversal that evening. She was the mother/therapist and I was an impatient child displaying a lack of empathy and support for her emotions. Kids can be quite humbling.

In order to provide "empathy lessons" to children, parents should prepare children to manage emotional difficulties offering a valuable education for successful functioning. I believe that life's "real moments" provide vital opportunities for children to experience sadness, loss, rejection, pain, humiliation, embarrassment, frustration, failure, etc. preparing them for adulthood. Allowing a child to make mistakes, face natural consequences for their behavior, and feel negative emotions will not harm your child (unless these consequences are abusive in nature). Allowing your child to feel hunger, a loss of privilege, sadness, discomfort, embarrassment, and other emotions not often depicted on Sesame Street will provide them with skills to manage their emotions – both positive and negative. After all, how can one learn to be empathetic if they are constantly protected from the realities of emotional life? Any individual will struggle to offer empathy if they have not personally experienced a vast array of emotions.

Life experiences offer numerous opportunities to develop a child's empathy. For example, teaching a child how to behave at a funeral; volunteering at homeless shelters, nursing homes, hospitals, and orphanages; visiting someone in the hospital; caring for someone who is bedridden or ill; donating food to a food pantry; mourning the loss of a cherished pet; comforting a friend who is sad; teaching a younger sibling a cherished skill; writing letters to family and friends; exposing them to individuals with physical and mental handicaps, etc... All of these experiences offer parents opportunities to "teach" their children how to face emotions in a healthy, unrepressed fashion preparing them for life's larger disappointments and negative experiences.

Bottom line: It's okay for kids to feel sad, bad, and mad. Without these feelings, they would not understand why feeling jolly, good, and happy were so important to a healthy emotional life.

Back to the Program...

In terms of building empathy using this program, offer your client the opportunity to portray the Mom or Dad role within the social story. Simply asking an individual to image and experience another's perspective will expand their understanding while offering a small dose of reality. The goal remains to create flexibility within their perception of emotions while developing their ability to emote more comfortably in a broader range of social situations.

Once you have completed the visualization and role play of a social story, the remaining step is to begin reversing roles. Ask your client to pick a character within the story they would like to enact. Suggest your client play an adult role within the story, while you choose a child's role. This will empower them by positioning yourself in a submissive role. Allowing them a "one up" position allows them to tip the power scales feeling in control of the social exchange. Additionally, your portrayal of the child's role in a social scenario will *allow you an opportunity* to empathize with the feelings of vulnerability and powerlessness accompanying childhood.

If time allows, switch roles as often as you desire. Or, role play a bit and record which characters you have played and continue role-playing this scenario during the next session. If the story contains rich examples for realistic discovery, it may warrant several role-reversals to process the breadth of emotional information.

Sample Dialogue: (Therapist and Adolescent Girl)
Roles are again chosen from the story in the previous section; however, with an alternative age and gender of the client.

Therapist: "Now that we've role played this story with you as Billy and me as the Mom, I want to change things up a little. I would like for you to choose another character to act out. Choose someone very different from yourself. The goal is to learn about others and their feelings as we learn about ourselves. Who would you like to play?"

Client: "I think I will try and play the Mom. I think it will be fun to act as a parent for a while."

Therapist: "I think that is a great idea - you can feel what it is like to discipline a child for a moment. Ready?"

Client: "I am ready."

Therapist: "(Acting as Billy) Mom, I don't understand why you are so mad at me! Sally was not paying attention and because she was being such a klutz, she totally ruined all of your pictures. I thought you would be mad too!"

Client: "(Acting as Mom) I am not happy that Sally broke my pictures, but I am more upset that you yelled at her. You really hurt her feelings."

Therapist:	"What is the big deal? She yells at me all of the time! I don't understand why you are protecting her! I swear sometimes you guys love her more than you love me."
Client:	"That's not true! Your Dad and I love you both the same. Sally is your little sister and you need to show her how she is supposed to act."
Therapist:	"It is so unfair! It seems like I always get into trouble and she gets away with everything! I'm always disappointing you - I can't do anything right!"
Client:	"It's OK to be frustrated, but you shouldn't take that out on your sister. You do things right a lot and you don't disappoint us all of the time."
Therapist:	"I guess I shouldn't have yelled and tattled on Sally like that. Maybe if I want to be treated like the older brother, I should act like one. Next time, I will be nicer if something like this happens. I don't like to hurt Sally's feelings."
Client:	"Maybe you should tell Sally you are sorry, just to make sure that she knows how you feel."
Therapist:	"Ok, I am sorry Sally for yelling at you. I should've been nicer about you making a mistake. I didn't mean to hurt your feelings."
Client:	"That is very nice Billy. I couldn't have said it better myself!"

This dialogue shows a level of emotional sophistication that may be witnessed within your older or more advanced clients. However, as time and practice occurs, it is not farfetched to expect this level of emotional understanding from your younger clients (although it may be verbalized with less sophistication). Your client's abilities will develop in accordance with their language and comprehension development. All children advance at different rates and in various ways. There are no specific "roadmaps" or shortcuts that can be followed arriving at the final destination. One must simply stimulate imagery, language, and emotional knowledge until an individual develops accordingly.

In order to portray a more realistic version of this task, the following dialogue has been included demonstrating some of the "snags" encountered when a younger (or newer) client attempts to express their feelings. This next dialogue allows the therapist the opportunity to direct the client back to the visualization process vital to ensuring comprehension and retention of the social concepts being developed.

Sample Dialogue: *(Therapist and Adolescent Girl just beginning therapy who lacks both language and imagery required to comprehend this scenario).*

Therapist:	"Now that we've role played this story with you as Billy and me as the Mom, I want to change things up a little. I would like for you to choose another character to act out. I encourage you to choose someone that is very different from yourself. The goal is to learn about others and their feelings as we learn about ourselves. Who would you like to play?"
Client:	"Maybe I should play Sally."

Therapist:	"Sally does seem like a good role to play because it matches more of your role within your own family. However, this time, I would like for you to play the Mom and I will play Billy. That way you can feel what its like to parent for a moment."
Client:	"I guess, but I think that'll be really hard."
Therapist:	"It is hard to act as someone very different from what we know. I sometimes have a hard time playing a child because I'm getting so old! (*Smile...wink*) But, I think it's really important we both try to understand how others may feel in different situations. Does that make sense?"
Client:	"It does. I just may not know what to say."
Therapist:	"That's perfectly OK because there's not a right or wrong to this. I will be here to help you with your words if you need me to, okay?"
Client:	"Okay, as long as we can stop and I can get some help."
Therapist:	"Absolutely! That is why I'm here. Okay, let's get started. (Acting as Billy). Mom, I don't understand why you are so mad at me! Sally was not paying attention and because she was being such a klutz, she totally ruined all of your pictures. I thought you would be mad too!"
Client:	"Klutz? What is that?"

Therapist:	"I want you to imagine how Sally ran into Billy when he was holding the box of pictures. What do you see?"
Client:	"I see Sally not paying attention and running right into him because she's not looking straight ahead. Is that what klutz means?"
Therapist:	"I like your image and to be more specific, a klutz is a not so nice word for someone who is uncoordinated and often runs into things, trips, etc. Do you know anyone like that?"
Client:	"I can actually be like that sometimes! But, I hate it when people say that I always mess stuff up."
Therapist:	"I agree. It's not fun to be reminded of our mistakes. Do you think Billy is being very nice when he calls Sally a klutz?"
Client:	"No, he's not. Okay, I know what to say now. (Acting as the Mom). Billy, it's not nice to call your sister that."
Therapist:	"That's a great start. Let me repeat my statement and then you can talk to Billy about your feelings about Sally breaking the pictures. I said: 'Mom, I don't understand why you are so mad at me! Sally was not paying attention and because she was being such a klutz, she totally ruined all of your pictures. I thought you would be mad too!'"
Client:	(Acting as Mom) "I wish Sally had not broken my pictures. But, I don't think you

	should call her names and yell at her."
Therapist:	"Good job! (Acting as Billy again). What is the big deal? She yells at me all of the time! I don't understand why you always protect her! I swear sometimes you guys love her more than you love me."
Client:	(Talking to the therapist). "I don't know what to say. Should I say something about how we love him too?"
Therapist:	"That is a very good question. I want you to picture this scene for a minute. Can you tell me how you think Billy is feeling?"
Client:	"I see him as angry because he thinks his parents are picking on him and letting Sally get away with breaking the pictures."
Therapist:	"Very good! I agree with that. I think that Billy might also be feeling a bit hurt and wanting reassurance from his parents that he's loved. So, as the parent, what do you think would be the most important feeling to talk about with Billy? You are a big sister, right? What would you like your parents to talk about with you first if you got into trouble with one of your little brothers?"
Client:	"Well, I hate it when my parents ignore how I feel and just try and make me think their way. Sometimes I wish they could understand how I feel. If my little brother does something wrong, he barely gets into trouble. But, if I do something wrong, it's a huge deal! Sometimes I feel like they love

him more too."

Therapist: "I am so glad you are able to share your feelings - that is very insightful. It is often difficult to be the older sibling because parents expect you to behave more responsibly. I want you to use your own experiences and try and talk with Billy in a way that you wish your Mom might do with you. Does that help you to picture this scene and act it out?"

Client: "Yeah, I think so. It's hard to picture how both Billy and the Mom should feel and act. This is really hard!"

Therapist: "You are right. It is hard to think about more than one person's perspective. But the good news is that the more we do this over time, the easier it'll be for you. I don't want you to focus on the saying the 'perfect' thing, just try and keep the scene pictured in your head and deal with the feelings that come up, okay?"

Client: "Okay. Here I go. (Acting as the Mom) Billy, it sounds like you're really mad and hurt. I want you to know that we love you and Sally the same. Sometimes being the big brother is really hard because we expect more from you than we do from her."

Therapist: "Great job! (Acting as Billy) That is so unfair Mom! You don't really care how I feel. You're only worried about Sally. I get tired of always getting into trouble – she gets away with everything!"

Client:	"Maybe you do get into trouble more often, but we think you can do more because you're older. Sally doesn't get away with everything. This was an accident."
Therapist:	"Fine, Mom. You just don't get it. Whatever!"
Client:	"I do get it. I don't want you or Sally to feel hurt. I think you should learn to control your temper."
Therapist:	"Yeah, I know."
Client:	"Maybe you should apologize to your sister."
Therapist:	"Ok, I'm sorry for hurting your feelings and yelling at you. There – are you satisfied Mom?"
Client:	"Yes, thank you."
Therapist:	(No longer acting as Billy). "You did a great job with that. See? Was that so bad?"
Client:	"Actually that was pretty fun. It was harder than I thought it would be to act as the parent. I figured I would yell at Billy and we'd be done! But, I guess it takes more than that to really teach your kid."
Therapist:	"You stated that very well. Parenting is difficult and requires a lot of energy. Sometimes finding the right words can be a challenge, but I think you did a nice job and set a fine example for many parents out there."

Step Four: Discussion and Critical Thinking Skills

Once the role-reversal task is completed, a discussion of the roles enacted should ensue. This may occur naturally upon the cessation of each role-play scenario, or you may create it as a more "formal" task. Discussing differences amongst the roles illuminates various perspectives individuals take throughout their lives.

For example, a mother will perceive the world quite differently than her children and vice versa. Additionally, when individuals step outside of their gender boundaries, they often catch a glimpse of the world through the eyes of the opposite sex. As one experiences alternative life roles through contrived exposure (such as this exercise), or life experience, their comprehension of emotional and social knowledge becomes diversified. Diversification may improve flexibility in thought, decision-making skills, and empathy.

When discussing the various roles portrayed with your client, be sure to ask questions stimulating a deeper level of cognitive and emotional processing. In education, these types of questions are referred to as H.O.T.S. (Higher Order Thinking Skills) questions, critical thinking skills, or Bloom's Taxonomy.

Bloom's Taxonomy is one approach to critical thinking involving a hierarchical structure of cognitive processing. It includes six domains creating a progression from simplistic critical thinking to complex analysis. Bloom's first category "Knowledge" defines, recalls, or recognizes the information presented.[2] The ability to obtain or recall knowledge-based information is the lowest level of cognitive processing, but pinnacle for applying higher order thinking.

When applying Bloom's category of "Knowledge" to the social stories, these questions center upon the What/Who/When type. For example: 1) What happened to this character? 2) What did he or she say? 3) What emotional response did the other person elicit? 4) When did that occur? 5) Who expressed sadness?

Bloom's second category "Comprehension" involves understanding the material's meaning sufficiently to discuss, explain, interpret, and predict its contents.[1,3,4] Comprehension is a crucial stepping stone to obtaining application skills regarding the material learned. These questions include the How/Why type. For example: 1) Why did the boy become angry with his mother? 2) How did the father show his love for his daughter? 3) I wonder why the sister threw her shoe at the dog?

Bloom's third cognitive domain "Application" applies learned theories by solving problems using required skills or knowledge.[1,4] This level of processing may go beyond the social story and include questions such as: 1) I wonder what you might have done in a similar situation? 2) I wonder how that might have affected your life if you were the father in that story? 3) How do you think this situation might occur in real life?

Bloom's fourth domain "Analysis" breaks down information into parts, draws conclusions, analyzes relationships between parts, evaluates the relevancy of the information, and recognizes when faulty thinking or assumptions have occurred.[1,3] As one moves up Bloom's hierarchy of critical thinking, the type of questioning requires a deeper level of thinking. This type of questioning may not be appropriate for younger clients; however, adolescent and adult clients (and more emotionally sophisticated youths) may benefit from this level of questioning by offering the opportunity to challenge issues within the story. For example, one might ask: 1) Does this story seem relevant to your life, why or why not? 2) How might this story have ended differently? What type of ending would you offer the story? 3) Are assumptions being made in this story regarding the mother's behavior? 4) Do you find this scenario to be logical and realistic? Why or why not?

Bloom's fifth cognitive domain "Synthesis" creatively uses prior information to produce a new outcome by formulating a new pattern, structure, experiment, or classification.[3,1] To exemplify, questions following this level of thinking might state: 1) Taking into account your own experiences, how might you have rewritten the dialogue in this story? 2) When considering your life and experiences with your parents, how might you have portrayed those characters? Would you have altered their display of emotions? 3) How might you have changed the mood and events within the story?

Bloom's final domain "Evaluation" compares and discriminates between ideas, makes choices based upon reasoned argument, and judges the material using personal values offering an end product with a given purpose.[3,4] These types of questions may include: 1) Upon personal reflection, do you feel that the character's emotions were valid? Why or why not? 2) Now that we have explored the various emotions and social issues within the story, what are your opinions about the events that transpired? 3) We have discussed rewriting the ending of the story to fit your personal experiences. In your opinion, how do you feel your ending to the story demonstrates more realism?

Step Five: Empathy Exercises

As a therapist in training, we were taught that infamous "therapist" question: "How does that make you feel?" Although the phrase has become clichéd and indeed sounds a bit cheesy, the idea behind this line of questioning remains sound. Empathy is a staple concept holding the world of emotion and social understanding together. Over the years, I have found that I truly help others when comprehending their perspective.

People belong to various cultures, ethnicities, age groups, socio-economic classes, genders, educational levels, etc. Therefore, I believe it is vital to consider a person's values and culture within the therapy room gaining a comprehensive understanding of their social and emotional needs. Not everyone desires to express themselves openly, nor do all cultures condone emotionally open exchanges. I concern myself with acquiring this knowledge because I do not wish to falsely assume emotional displays and desires equal that of my own.

By truly listening to your clients needs, you will foster a feeling of acceptance and understanding. Individuals who are members of an oppressed minority group may present unique issues when in therapy. Educating yourself regarding their experiences and needs will be *your job*. It is not their job to convert themselves to *your set* of values and cultural norms. Therefore, if you provide therapeutic intervention to an individual of a different race, culture, religion, or some form of affiliation disparate from your own, research these differences and gain the knowledge required to offer therapy based upon their needs.

Why do people feel misunderstood? Why don't others seem to "get" their frame of reference? Why do some individuals display difficulty relating to others allowing for mutual understanding? The answers to these questions may lie within a person's deficit when comprehending social and emotional information. However, some of these issues may relate to a person's experiences of discrimination – they could very well be misunderstood due to real differences between themselves and the majority.

It is your task to tease these issues apart and consider the possibility that your client may have intact social and emotional knowledge; however, it may differ dramatically from your own. Discuss these issues with your client to determine if a social deficit exists, or if they are truly subjugated to acts of prejudice and bias within their environment creating misunderstanding from those around them.

Engaging in a few empathy exercises does not necessarily presume a person will suddenly possess superior empathy skills. However, it is a good start. Empathy can be practiced and honed, as one makes an effort to practice kindness and understanding. Some people are blessed with natural patience, understanding, kindness, etc. while others have to work harder to earn these virtues. Empathy may be approached in the same manner. By asking yourself to improve upon your empathy skills and creating the impetus to change, you may find yourself pausing before verbalizing a judgmental or critical comment. As you improve upon your empathy abilities, you will model these behaviors for those around you - both personally and professionally.

To initialize empathetic thinking, include "I wonder" statements in your verbalizations. These statements accomplish several goals simultaneously. As previously mentioned, when working with children, it is helpful to take a "one down" position allowing the power balance to shift in the child's favor. This includes a change not only in your language, but the choices and behaviors you make in session.

I often act a bit "clueless" versus behaving as the "expert" when building rapport and trust with my clients. Socratic dialogue is helpful because it forces you to listen in lieu of presenting yourself as the all-knowing adult. Kids tire of being lectured and patronized by adults. Hence, I exert an effort to model a relationship of respect and trust whilst engaging with children.

I remind myself that children are not adults, do not think like adults, and should therefore not be expected to behave like adults. This allows me to consider what is socially, emotionally, and cognitively appropriate for their age. In many instances, I work with children who are chronologically older than their developmental age. My job often involves lessening the gap between these two ages. By verbalizing and addressing their emotions at their current mental age (versus their chronological age), you will forge a greater level of trust and understanding within the therapeutic relationship.

Your have engaged your client in natural empathy exercises through role-reversals and discussions regarding these roles. However, the actual "formal" empathy exercises have been posed as questions. Empathy can be taught and learned, but does not involve the same form of skill acquisition as learning to tie one's shoes. It requires numerous and varied learning experiences to truly "hit home" the idea that empathy is a method of thinking and a choice one makes when responding to others. For example, it can be taught when shopping in the grocery store and a child sees an individual who is injured, handicapped, elderly, or different in any way from themselves. A parent may state to their child, "People are different from each another and these differences create variety in life – so, we need to accept others for their differences and try to understand what they might be going through. I wonder what it would be like to live your life in a [wheelchair, with one leg, deaf, blind, mentally retarded, Autistic, deformed, with Alzheimer's, alone, oppressed, sad, etc…]?"

It is an ongoing conversation between parent and child throughout the child's development. As adults, I think we might benefit from empathy "tune ups" reminding ourselves the world is composed of varied individuals with alternative thoughts, behaviors, experiences, and feelings from our own.

Some of the questions you may pose to any individual with whom you wish to buffer their empathy skills are as follows:
1) I wonder why they think that way?
2) I wonder why they said that?
3) I wonder what emotion they are feeling?
4) I wonder how they would feel if _____?
5) I wonder how they feel when people say _____?
6) I wonder what would happen if I (or they) reacted like _____?
7) I wonder how I would feel if they said that?
8) I wonder what it would be like to experience life the way they do?
9) Can you imagine how it might feel to be [deaf, blind,

handicapped, deformed, disabled, mentally ill, mentally retarded, etc...]?
10) I wonder what we could say or do to show that person we understand them?
11) I wonder what others can do or say to show a person they are loved?
12) I wonder what types of behaviors would show that we care for another?

In addition to empathy, the idea of anticipating and planning for future social and emotional situations is important when managing ones emotions. If you realize that you are going to be involved in social situation where an individual may be disparate from your own child, you may wish to "prep" your child warding off any inappropriate remarks to that individual. Even with good intention and preparation, a child may speak their mind, as children so often do.

However, it never hurts to prepare children for novel situations arming them with a newfound understanding and to decrease the shock value of a new situation. To exemplify, I might state to my own daughters in the car on the way to a friend's house, "Ok, girls, we are going over to the Jones' house tonight for dinner. They have 3 kids and one of their children, Mary, is in a wheelchair. She had an accident when she was very young and can no longer use her legs for walking. So, when we get there, I want you to remember to treat her as you do the other children by talking to her and including her in your play. Please do not stare, point, or say anything that might hurt her feelings. Okay? I wonder what life would be like to be in a wheelchair? Can you guys tell me what you imagine for that?"

Children between the ages of 3 and 4 may begin to understand the concept of hurting another's feelings (and start to exhibit a small sense of guilt by the age of 4). You may begin to have these types of conversations with them prior to this age. For example, I might state to my children, "I wonder how she feels when you take her toy away? Look, she's crying, I think she's sad because you took her toy. Let's give her toy back and ask her if she wants to share."

These types of responses (as opposed to getting angry, or punishing the child for their behavior) will instill a greater sense of emotional responsibility for their behavior. "I wonder how you would feel if she took your toy away when you are playing with it? Would you feel sad too?" Socratic questioning often contains the same content as a good parental lecture; however, with the added bonus of "chin scratching" allowing the child an opportunity for experiential learning. Often, the "I wonder" question and answer sessions are not as quickly met with the glazed expression of "selective hearing" many children learn when parents begin to launch into a lecture. But, then again, one doesn't want to ask for small miracles! As a parent, you will at some point be ignored. As a therapist, this holds true as well.

Regardless, once you have had these conversations a few times, they may at some point become unnecessary. This will come to fruition as you continue to encourage and acknowledge your child's positive emotional and social behaviors. For example, "I liked how you hugged Aunt Betsy at the end of dinner. She seemed really happy when you did that." Or, for older kids you might say, "I really appreciated the way you shook Uncle Frank's hand before we left their house. That was really a polite and mature thing to do."

I have found that over the years of working with children, one of the strongest positive reinforcers a parent or therapist possesses is their ability to acknowledge and praise a child in a timely fashion for their appropriate behaviors. Like sugar or salt, too much or too little can make the food taste yucky. Similarly with praise, too much or too little (or at the inappropriate time) can be ineffective. I have learned not to be "over the top" with praise by stating it with a warm and pleased tone of voice while ensuring that I verbalize my praise when the behavior occurs. Here are a few examples of positive praise when reinforcing social and emotional behaviors:

"I liked how you asked your sister to play with you instead of telling her to. She seemed happy that you were giving her a choice."

"It was nice how you told that boy at the park that you did not want to play on the swings. You said that in a way that did not hurt his feelings."

"I liked how you looked your brother in the eye when you told him that hitting you was not nice and that you would not play with him if he acted that way. That was a very grown-up way to speak."

"I think you did a good job when you told your friend that you could not meet her at the mall. She seemed upset at first, but you showed that you cared about her feelings. She seemed happy by the time you guys had finished your conversation. You handled that very well."

"Thank you for asking me nicely for a snack. I really liked how you didn't demand anything, but said please and thank you."

"I noticed that you did not seem pleased with tonight's dinner at Grandma's house. I think it was really good of you not to tell her that you didn't like the food. Sometimes, we have to keep some things to ourselves so we don't hurt others. You did just that!"

"Thank you for working so hard today in session. I could tell at times you were frustrated, but you did not complain and continued to work really hard – nice job!"

Group and Family Format
Note: Please see Chapter 18 for greater detail involving family role play.

Step One: Reading, Exploring, & Imaging the Story
Read the story to the family or group. Explore the initial content and emotions of the characters within the story, while ensuring comprehension of vocabulary terms. You may decide to use the "Round Robin" technique within your group when building imagery for the story. Or, you may ask one person to verbalize their images and have others help as needed. Use choice and contrast questioning developing imagery for the social scene. Reread the story if necessary ensuring complete imagery and comprehension.

Step Two: Role Play
Ask your family or group to choose roles within the story. Have the family or group act out the scenario allowing an opportunity to gain comfort with the expression of various emotions. Answer any questions arising throughout the process. Model certain roles and behaviors and ask the group to mimic your social modeling. Use the group to teach one another and minimize your role within this scenario. Allow the group or family to become more independent within their roles.

Step Three: Role-Reversal
Ask the group or family to switch roles with one another in order to build empathy and understanding of various roles people portray within their social environment.

Step Four: Discussion & Critical Thinking Skills
Ask Who, What, When, Why, and How questions pertaining to the story stimulating critical thinking skills for your family or group. Apply Bloom's taxonomy using questions based upon one's knowledge, comprehension, application, analysis, synthesis, and evaluation of the story.

Allow group members an opportunity to share personal experiences and learn from one another.

Step Five: Empathy Exercises

Ask the group "I wonder" questions pertaining to the story to further emphasize the understanding of various perspectives. Use positive praise when witnessing the group's use of empathy. This is an appropriate time to practice empathy skills by group role-playing personal experiences shared by the group.

Additional Group "Themes" for Group Imagery, Education, & Discussion:

- Coping Mechanisms
- Anger Management
- Conflict Resolution
- Organizational Skills
- Scheduling and Planning
- Time Management
- Cognitive Distortions
- Sex Education
- Current Events
- Social Conflicts
- Discrimination
- Prejudice
- Sexual Appropriateness
- Flexibility vs. Rigidity

Review of Imaging Social Stories and Role Play Steps

1) Step One: Reading, Exploring, & Imaging the Story

- Read the story to your client.
- Explore the initial content and emotions of the characters within the story.
- Ensure comprehension of vocabulary terms.
- Use choice and contrast questioning building imagery for the social scene.
- Reread the story (if necessary) ensuring imagery and comprehension.

2) Step Two: Role Play

- Choose roles within the story.
- Act out the scenario allowing an opportunity to gain comfort with the expression of various emotions.

3) Step Three: Role-Reversal

- Switch or reverse roles with your client building empathy and understanding of the various roles people portray within their social environment.

4) Step Four: Discussion & Critical Thinking Skills

- Ask Who, What, When, Why, and How questions stimulating critical thinking skills.

- Apply Bloom's taxonomy using questions based upon knowledge, comprehension, application, analysis, synthesis, and evaluation of the story.

5) Step Five: Empathy Exercises

- Ask "I wonder" questions emphasizing alternative perspectives.

- Use positive praise when witnessing the use of empathy skills.

~14~
Imaging Emotional Discrepancies

The ability to observe socially and emotionally inconsistent information within one's environment is a powerful reinforcement to an individual's learning. Similar to the game in children's magazines instructing you to find "What's wrong in this picture?" we can look within our surroundings observing social incongruities. The intention of this process is not to create hyper-critical individuals pointing out the social and emotional floundering of others. But rather, to utilize and apply emotional intelligence throughout daily life creating connections with others based upon sound social and emotional tenets.

This program has offered several methods for developing EI skills – through role play, vocabulary building, and imagery building. Additionally, one may present emotional discrepancies, or sentences containing social or emotional incongruities, to build upon one's imagery. Sentences containing emotionally inconsistent information force an individual to discover what is "strange" or "awkward" about that sentence by imaging its content and comparing that image to their knowledge of what "should happen" in that social scenario.

Emotional discrepancies may be obvious, or subtle,

dependent upon the needs and developmental age of the child. I have created several within Appendix 5; however, I encourage you to use personal examples from your client's lives (jot down ideas during your sessions as they arise). Personal experience and current events are powerful tools providing salience to an individual versus examples less pertinent to one's life. We learn effectively through our own experiences versus experiences of others, or irrelevant examples.

When creating emotional discrepancy sentences, use emotions expressed in contradictory ways than how the person should feel. Do we always express our anger, frustration, jealousy, fear, sadness, etc. in socially appropriate ways? Or, are we capable of taking out our emotions upon others and doing harm because we lack self awareness? The idea is to determine how others express their emotions and whether those behavioral expressions are appropriate in that situation. This task is fraught with personal opinions and values, as emotional expression varies across individuals. However, many would agree that taking out negative emotions upon others in a hurtful manner can create strife. This task is designed to create images for both appropriate and inappropriate emotional behaviors building a source of social comparison for your client.

As with many of the other tasks presented, the focus of this task is to boost visual imagery. Therefore, the majority of your language should encourage visualization. By using your language to direct their thinking process, you can aid their imaging by merely asking, "What do you [see, image, picture, imagine, visualize] for that?" If you ask an individual what they hear, they will attune their senses to the auditory information being filtered through their sensory system. Similarly if you ask an individual what they feel, taste, see, or image, they will direct their attention and focus to that particular mode of sensory input. Your language is directive and integral to the therapeutic process, as you focus and hone their attention to their imagery.

Emotional discrepancy sentences promote the comprehension of humor to individuals presenting language deficits. Individuals with expressive or receptive language issues often demonstrate weakness within their ability to comprehend humor. Consider how humor is processed within the brain. In order to comprehend a joke and find it humorous, one must be able to image the discrepancy in the information provided comparable to what occurs in reality. For example, the joke might read: "Question: When is a car not a car? Answer: When it turns into a garage."

In order to find that joke amusing (to the extent that joke is actually funny), one should image a car physically morphing into a garage versus a car driving into the garage. In this way, the discrepancy between what should occur and what did occur seems humorous. However, if one were not able to image proficiently, or comprehend the language within the joke, they would not find the joke funny because the discrepancy between what happened in the joke and what *should happen* in real life was not imaged; therefore, the joke's punch line is lost.

You have heard the saying, "In one ear and out the other." This statement infers that language can be physically heard, but if not imaged and processed, the content of the message is lost. Imagine the frustration experienced by someone in a social situation when others laugh at a joke they cannot understand.

Step One: Read and Image the Emotional Discrepancy

Focus on the visualization process throughout this task. Set the task up by telling the client you will be asking them to image the sentence discovering what seems "off" or "strange" about the sentence. The first sample dialogue demonstrates the use of a concrete verbal discrepancy in order to practice this concept with your client. It will be easier for an individual to image concrete information;

therefore, you may wish to practice several sentences with no emotional and social content focusing solely upon the imagery process. An additional sample dialogue is presented demonstrating a discrepancy with emotional content after the introduction of *Step 3: Creating New Sentences.*

After you have introduced the task, read your first sentence to the client. Appendix 5 contains emotional discrepancy statements for your use, or you may desire to create your own. Either way, it is important to choose simplistic and high imagery statements at the onset of the task. Remember to read slowly and use appropriate intonation maximizing interest for the listener. A demonstration of this step is as follows:

Sample Dialogue: (Therapist and Young Boy)

Therapist:	"I want to read you a sentence that has something silly or strange about it. I want you to use your pictures in your mind to see if you can figure out what that strange thing is. It will be your job to listen to my words, make a movie in your head, and catch the silly thing that I am saying. After I am finished reading this sentence to you, I want you to tell me what you imagined."
Client:	"You want me to tell you what's funny about your sentence? Okay, sounds easy to me."
Therapist:	"Good - here's your first statement. *Johnny rode the bus into the school building today.*"
Client:	"Hmm...There's nothing really silly about that. I ride the bus into school all the time."
Therapist:	"You're right - You are able to ride your bus

to school everyday. However, let's check and see if Johnny rode the bus to school or something else. *Johnny rode the bus into the school building today'* Can you picture where the school bus is actually going?"

Client: "Well, all I can think of is that Johnny was riding the bus. So, I still don't see what's so funny about that sentence. This is not fun; can we do something else now?"

Therapist: "I understand this may not seem that fun. However, it's important that we can make good pictures in our heads to see if others are making sense. Let's see if I can help you a bit with this sentence, and then we can move on. How old do you picture Johnny to be?"

Client: "About my age, you know, 10. He's riding on a big yellow school bus, like the one I ride on."

Therapist: "That's great! I can picture that too. Where do you see Johnny's bus going in your picture?"

Client: "I see him riding the bus to a big brick school building."

Therapist: "Now you're cooking. Let's check and see if he rides the bus to the school, or does something a little different. *Johnny rode the bus into* (emphasize with your voice) *the school building today.* Can you picture Johnny's bus driving into the school building? I bet that would be quite a sight to see the bus go through the building!"

Client: "Oh, now I get it. The funny thing is that the bus drove into the building, like crashed into it! I wasn't picturing that part. That would be very bad for the kids on the bus!"

Therapist: "I agree. Now, you're really starting to make some good images in your mind. "

Note to Parents:
Parents can utilize time with their children promoting the observation of social and emotional discrepancies. The more often these issues are directly addressed, the more likely a child will decipher the appropriate social information within a given situation. The grocery store is a great forum for social observation. If parenting young children, placing them in the grocery cart for "a ride" is a great way to give them an elevated vantage point to witness social exchanges throughout the aisles. In this fashion, they are a bit removed from social interaction and given the freedom to observe others.

You can have conversations about people's behavior (not directly within earshot), ask for interpretations regarding that behavior, and ask your child how they might behave or feel in that given situation. My youngest daughter (3 years old at the time) always wanted to know: "Why is the baby crying?"; "Why did that Mommy get mad?"; "Is that boy getting into trouble?"; "Can I go touch the baby and make her feel better?"

No topic is ever too small to instill a bit of social and emotional knowledge. These "little" conversations throughout the day may seem trivial to an adult brain; however, these topics are novel and important to young minds. Children receiving a consistent flow of social and emotional information may stockpile this knowledge creating social measuring sticks to compare emotional discrepancies. As children witness social exchanges in conjunction with parental explanations and discussions, they create mental pictures of the social issue witnessed and can therefore, recall it in future situations when information challenges their previous experiences. By using language to buffer their imagery of the social experience, a parent can enhance this process. You might ask: "What do you picture that caused the baby to cry? Can you imagine what might have angered that Mommy? Can you think of a reason that you might cry? I wonder how that Mommy will make that baby feel better?"

It may seem a bit over-the-top when first discussing these issues so directly with your children. We are eager to instill cognitive skills within our young children, such as letters, numbers, colors, shapes, etc...Why not buffer their emotional and social intelligence directly as well? Why not directly teach them what a frustrated versus angry face looks like? Why not offer them the direct knowledge regarding an improved method for communicating their anger in a social situation? (I promote the use of "magic breaths" to calm children when they feel anger or frustration).

According to Daniel Goleman's book, *Social Intelligence*, humans are hard-wired to comprehend social information processing this information faster than our conscious mind registers. He terms this process the "low road" of information processing because it is faster and less accurate than the rational and logical prefrontal cortex. Before we are able to "think" through a given social situation, our brain has already processed emotional cues and made a quick judgment. Our slower cognitive brain eventually catches up rationalizing the perceived social information. In essence, we are hard-wired to receive and respond to social and emotional cues throughout our environment.

If we offer children the opportunity to observe and interpret social information employing the visual part of their brain, they may retain this knowledge creating more fluid functioning. Our biggest error with children is the assumption they will "pick up" social and emotional information independently without guidance and direct stimulation. As we do not expect children to learn to tie shoe laces independently; we should not expect them to comprehend social nuances of behavior without our guidance. Social and emotional understanding may be hard-wired into our genetic code; however, a large portion of these skills remain to be learned and understood.

Step Two: Hone Imagery and Discussion

Once the sentence has been read, your task will be to hone the imagery ensuring your client is truly "seeing" the information provided. The use of choice and contrast questions should be implemented when helping further develop their image. For example, "Is the man tall or short? Was he laughing or smiling? Did the girl walk or run?"

Discuss the discrepancies within the scenario once you perceive the sentence to be sufficiently imaged. For example, one discrepancy might read: "The man's dog died, so he just laughed and laughed." This sentence is simplistic, but will help illustrate the point. Ensure your client is imaging a man and a dog. "Where are the man and the dog? Over a grave? At the veterinarian's office? Are they imaging the man laughing?"

Once an image is established, you can discuss the appropriate emotional response in this situation. If your client is imaging automatically, they will hear this statement and may laugh or immediately correct it. If they begin to correct all of the statements and verbalize the appropriate emotional and social responses rather quickly, they are ready to move on from this task, or be offered increasingly more complex scenarios.

Try to create subtle social and emotional discrepancies requiring a higher level of imaging and verbal comprehension to determine the discrepancy. For example, a more complicated discrepancy might read: "As the man walked past the woman, he caught her eyes with his own and held her gaze for a moment. The woman just knew that the man had no interest in her." This example shows a level of ambiguity requiring inference and conclusion drawing to ascertain the meaning behind this social exchange. Social ambiguity and vagueness will help your client create more intricate images when inferring the meaning and discrepancy within the sentence. For example, "What does it mean when strangers lock eyes? Does the fact that they are of the opposite sex matter to this social exchange? What cues were given to the woman to feel the man showed disinterest?"

Step Three: Creating New Sentences

Once your client has created images and discussed any social and emotional differences occurring, ask them to recreate the sentence so that it makes sense. In the case of the man with the deceased dog, your client should fix it to read: "The man's dog died, so he just cried and cried." Once again, this sentence is simplistic, but illustrates the method for this exercise. Correcting the sentence is as vital as imaging the discrepancy because it offers closure to the exercise presenting your client an opportunity to visualize a comparison between appropriate and inappropriate statements.

You may decide to write your own discrepancies using social and emotional themes requiring attention within your client's life. Where does your client harbor the greatest social difficulties? Is it at school with friends? With members of the opposite sex? In adult situations requiring dialogue? Where does your client demonstrate discomfort and trouble within their social world?

Use the emotional discrepancies task to provide your client with adequate imagery to view their social scenarios in greater depth. By analyzing these images and comparing them to alternative images, your client will build their ability to decipher these differences independently. The ability to image alternative choices in social situations may aid their future social interactions.

Sample Dialogue: (demonstrates Steps 1, 2, & 3 with Therapist and Adolescent Girl)

Therapist: "I am going to read you a sentence that may seem strange or 'off' in some way. Your job will be to make an image in your head and tell me how the sentence is silly. Understand?"

Client: "I think so. You want me to picture the sentence and tell you how it is silly."

Therapist: "Exactly. Here is your sentence: *Jackie was jealous of her friend's new boyfriend, so when she saw them together, she ignored them and walked past them quickly without saying 'Hello.'* What does that sentence make you image?"

Client: "Well, I see a teenage girl, about my age and she walks past a couple and doesn't stop."

Therapist: "That is a good start. Let's see if we can flush out the details a bit. Tell me more about what you image for her facial expressions and body language."

Client: "Well, I see the couple as happy and smiling. I see them hugging each other."

Therapist: "I can image that as well. Can you tell me more about the best friend? What type of facial expression might she show?"

Client: "Well, the sentence said that she was jealous, so I was seeing her walking by with her nose up in the air – kind of looking stuck up."

Therapist:	"Why might she look that way?"
Client:	"I think she is trying to blow off her friend because she is feeling jealous. She probably feels left out and ignored, so maybe she is mad about that."
Therapist:	"That is really good. I can picture that as well. Can you tell me more about her body language as she walks by?"
Client:	"I see her walking really quickly, like she doesn't see them. She's trying to play it cool, but she looks upset anyway."
Therapist:	"I like how you imagined her *trying* to look like nothing happened. How can you tell that she is upset?"
Client:	"Well, her arms and legs look stiff and I see her walking quickly with her head held high and her nose in the air. Her mouth also looks really tight, like she has her lips pressed together. Maybe she is trying not to cry?"
Therapist:	"You think that she might be upset?"
Client:	"I think she is upset about her friend with her new boyfriend and she might be ready to cry."
Therapist:	"Those are great observations. What about this sentence seems a little off to you?"
Client:	"Well, at first, I didn't think the sentence was strange at all because I have seen people get

mad at their friends for having a boyfriend. I have seen girls at school act this way towards their best friend."

Therapist: "I bet you are right. It seems like people can really get their feelings hurt when they perceive dating to interfere with a friendship. How would you improve this sentence to make Jackie's response more socially appropriate towards her friend?"

Client: "I think that it is wrong of her to feel jealous."

Therapist: "Jealousy may be an unfair emotion for her to feel. But, as you stated, often people get jealous of others' romantic interests. Can you think of some reasons why she might be feeling jealous?"

Client: "Well, she might feel as though her friend no longer will have time for her. Or, I think that sometimes girls get jealous of their friends' boyfriends because they don't have one."

Therapist: "I think those are both very nice interpretations. I would agree with you. Jealousy can be a complex emotion. Can you imagine a more socially appropriate response Jackie could've shown her friend?"

Client: "Well, Jackie probably should've stopped and spoken to her friend. Even if she was feeling jealous, it was rude of her to walk by and ignore them."

Therapist: "I agree with you. Even though Jackie may feel jealous, there are more appropriate ways

	to communicate that to her friend. I wonder if ignoring her friend will improve their relationship?"
Client:	"I think it will make it worse because now the other girl will be upset because she was ignored."
Therapist:	"I bet you are right. It does not feel good to be snubbed, or ignored. How might you reword this sentence to show a more appropriate social exchange?"
Client:	"I would say: Jackie felt jealous of her friend's new boyfriend, but said 'Hello' when she walked by to be polite."
Therapist:	"That is really good. Taking this one step further, if you were Jackie, how would you handle your feelings of jealousy towards your best friend's relationship? What might you say to her?"
Client:	"That would be really hard. But, I might tell her that I miss spending time with her and I feel left out because she spends all of her time with her boyfriend. I would tell her that I feel sad because we don't' spend as much time together."
Therapist:	"Wow! You really know how to express your feelings directly. I like how you talk about how you feel and do not blame her for her behavior. I think your best friend might respond by saying, 'I am sorry that I have not spent as much time with you. Maybe we can plan some time to spend together. I did not

	know that I hurt your feelings.' What would you say to her then?"
Client:	"I would tell her that we should plan some time to hang out together."
Therapist:	"You really did a great job with this scenario."

Group and Family Format

Step One: Read and Image the Emotional Discrepancy
Read the sentence to your family or group. You may decide to use the "Round Robin" technique and ask each member to verbalize a part of the imagery for the sentence, or ask one person to image the entire sentence having others add to the imagery as needed.

Step Two: Hone Imagery and Discussion
Help the family or group hone their image by using choice and contrast questioning flushing out the details of the sentence. Ensure all vocabulary terms are understood. Discuss the social or emotional discrepancies within the sentence. Make time for the group to brainstorm ideas regarding the appropriateness of the discrepancy and how they might go about changing the sentence.

Step Three: Creating New Sentences
Ask your family or group to verbalize methods of improvement regarding the social scenario and recreate the sentence to reflect greater social and emotional appropriateness. Create independence by offering less input and allowing time for the group to verbalize their thought processes.

Review of Imaging Emotional Discrepancy Steps

1) Step One: Read and Image the Emotional Discrepancy

- Read the sentence to your client and ask them to verbalize their imagery.

2) Step Two: Hone Imagery and Discussion

- Help the client create a more detailed image using choice/contrast questioning.

- Discuss the discrepancies within the sentence and how they are socially inappropriate.

3) Step Three: Creating New Sentences

- Ask the client to create a new sentence containing more socially and emotionally appropriate content.

- Allow them to verbalize thoughts regarding the improvement of this social scenario.

~15~
Mixed Bag of Emotions

Boosting the Mind's Eye is based upon clinical experience, research, and the trials and tribulations transpiring within professional life. The driving force behind this method of intervention derives its motivation from both parents and professionals requesting specific tasks developing a child's social and emotional comprehension.

Through the exploration of new treatment methods stimulating both their visualization and their social and emotional skills, new tasks were created serendipitously. Clients often discussed family, friends, and social issues as top priorities for therapeutic guidance. They were often asked to visualize "what if" endings to social conflicts facilitating the problem solving of socially appropriate behaviors. This proved helpful as they utilized the safety of the therapy room creating desirable or undesirable endings to their problems.

By processing emotional issues associated with a social mishap, while simultaneously creating choices for future behavior, we were able to instill the tools required for positive social engagement. Discussing and working through negative emotions associated with social situations, while developing language and imagery required when comprehending more complex information, created greater retention of these skills.

The brunt of our work was in abstract vocabulary development because many of my clients were "concrete thinkers" and did not truly comprehend abstract information. Hence, we spent time anchoring abstract concepts with concrete images. Pop-culture turned out to be helpful in these situations, as I often found myself using People magazine, or other periodicals illustrating individuals displaying a wide range of emotions and social situations.

Upon realizing the value in using as many varied images as possible, I cut out numerous photos and wrote down the associated emotion or social scenario on an index card. To create a fun exercise, I mixed all of the photos and verbal descriptions together in the same bag, asked the client to dump them out, and then match up the photos with the appropriate verbal description.

Step One: Cut, Tag, and Bag

A fun hands on instruction exercise includes taking family photos, magazines, newspapers, clip art, etc. and create your own "mixed bag" of emotions. Try and include body language and background information in your cut-outs providing more visual information pertinent to the social and emotional display.

Next, identify and write down the emotion or social scene portrayed on a blank index card, or slip of paper. Mix all of these photos and descriptions in a bag and ask your client to dump out the contents of the bag and match the photos with their proper descriptions. You may decide to limit the number of emotions or social scenarios within the bag dependent upon your client's language abilities, as well as emotional understanding.

To increase the level of difficulty, add extraneous emotional labels to the bag not depicted within the photos. This allows the client an opportunity to discriminate appropriate versus inappropriate emotional labels. By adding superfluous emotional descriptors, you will bolster the emotional discrepancy task they have just completed by using emotions already discussed.

Younger children (and older alike) may enjoy cutting out photos and creating "emotional murals" on poster board. They can affix both the pictures and emotional labels to the poster board creating any social or emotional theme discussed. This "cut and paste" exercise is a fun, concrete task helpful in the identification of social information.

Step Two: Story Time

Contingent upon the age and language abilities of your client, you may decide to create social stories about the magazine cut outs. I have found that clients may disagree with my emotional labels and may interpret the photo differently. I always welcome their interpretation, as some emotions are vague or ambiguous – therefore, is there truly a right or wrong? Relabeling the emotion in the photos allows them an opportunity to own the process and think critically regarding emotional information.

Ask your client to verbalize a story about these characters. Take turns creating portions of the story modeling creative thinking and verbalization of the social and emotional information presented.

Ask critical thinking skills questions pertinent to the stories created, such as: Who, What, When, Where, Why, How, and "I Wonder" questions stimulating deeper processing of the social information. Apply Bloom's Taxonomy examining their ability to verbalize knowledge, comprehension, application, analysis, synthesis, and evaluation of the social scenario.

Group and Family Format

Step One: Cut, Tag, and Bag

Cut out photos from magazines or other materials. Write down the corresponding emotions or social situations on slips of paper. Mix all of the photos and descriptions in a bag. Ask your family or group to dump the bag out and match up all of the photos with the descriptors. Remember to add in erroneous descriptors improving upon their emotional discrimination skills.

Ask group members to give one another feedback regarding the choices made when matching the photos with the descriptors. Allow each member to match the photos and descriptors. This is a fun "floor time" activity that allows everyone to be involved simultaneously. Therefore, you may wish to create a bigger bag dependent upon the size of the group.

Step Two: Story Time

Ask your family or group to make up a story for the photos. You may decide to go in a "Round Robin" format and have each member verbalize one sentence of the story and build upon each other's sentences. Or, you may decide to let each group member take turns making up the entire story.

Be sure to ask critical thinking skills questions, or Bloom's taxonomy developing a deeper level of comprehension regarding the depicted social scenes. Use time to foster group discussion promoting social learning within the group.

Review of Mixed Bag of Emotions Steps

1) **Step One: Cut, Tag, and Bag**

    - Cut out photos from magazines or other sources.

    - Write down corresponding emotional or social labels on slips of paper.

    - Mix all photos and descriptions in a bag.

    - Ask client to dump the bag and match the photos and descriptors.

    - Add in erroneous descriptors to improve discrimination skills.

2) **Step Two: Story Time**

    - Ask your client to make up a story for the photos.

    - Take turns creating the story together.

    - Ask critical thinking skills questions, or Bloom's taxonomy developing a deeper level of comprehension regarding the depicted social scenes.

~16~
Journaling Emotions

Where Have All the Writers Gone?
Clients displaying receptive, expressive, or mixed language deficits often demonstrate difficulty with written expression. Through therapeutic intervention, these individuals may improve upon their ability to express themselves verbally; however, their written expression often remains underdeveloped unless directly stimulated.

Written expression is a vital skill necessitating guidance and remediation. The responsibility to educate our children and develop their writing skills should fall upon us all – be it parents, educators, mental health professionals, tutors, mentors, administrators, etc. I have witnessed in awe at the deterioration of writing skills of American youth both personally and professionally. Regardless of age, grade level, type of education (public or private), or presence of a learning disability, the ability to write with fluency and organized expression is seriously lacking in this country. Because I do not wish to blame our educational models (I think society does that enough), I will merely make the blanketed statement that many children do not receive the quality or quantity of specialized writing time necessary to improve upon their skills.

Writing with fluency is an intricate process involving:

brainstorming, formulating main ideas and details, organization, grammar, punctuation, sequence, spelling, vocabulary, and creativity. In essence, it is an application of every academic skill humans are taught throughout their education. Therefore, the notion that this skill requires numerous instructional hours and practice should not be surprising. Writing skills instruction without specific feedback to the writer is not sufficient enough to create comprehensive writing abilities. Without teaching the editing process, as well as the "rewriting process," individuals will lack the application of critical thinking and improvement necessary for coherent writing.

I firmly believe the ability to proficiently edit one's written work is more crucial than the raw data and blurbs of language originally printed on paper. Without years of grueling editing experiences from teachers and professors scribbling the infamous "red ink" all over my papers, my writing skills would have been drastically stunted.

Teachers in public schools are often inundated with students and do not possess vast amounts of one-on-one time. Because time constraints are apparent in the classroom, parents should become more involved in this process. Parents may facilitate their children's writing skills by: reading through their child's writing; brainstorming with their children; asking critical thinking skills questions; helping edit their work; and discussing organizational skills when writing.

I continually feel surprise (and horror) at high school and college students struggling with the formulation of a main idea sentence from previously read material. In order to remediate this, we spend time reading passages, making images in our mind's eye, verbalizing main ideas, and writing those ideas on paper. Fluent visualization is required to conjure fluent thoughts on paper.

Fluidity, creativity, and higher order thinking skills are required to read a passage, digest the information, analyze its content, and write down one's ideas regarding that analysis. This skill is not one learned passively. It is an acquired, learned, practiced skill requiring instruction, feedback, and painstaking repetition on the part of the writer.

"Why – that sounds like a blast!" you might say. Sarcasm aside, writing is not always fun. It is often laborious, tedious, and creates mounds of frustration. Yet, the benefits of writing down one's thoughts in a coherent, logical, and somewhat stylish manner offer an individual a sense of accomplishment lasting a lifetime.

Let's Get Writing!
Asking your clients to write down their thoughts is one method of promoting additional writing time. Identified as "journaling," this process has been utilized for all ages as a source of emotional catharsis. In the past, when asking my clients to journal, I requested that they complete this task in the privacy of their homes. After all, the concept of a "diary" seems private and worthy of safe-guarding. However, I quickly realized that my clients were less likely to journal at home because they abhorred the writing process altogether. They were no more comfortable writing personal thoughts than a paper for school. In their mind, writing was writing and remained a scary and daunting task fraught with frustration and failure.

Through trial and tribulation, I discovered an intervention facilitating the recovery process of their "writing phobia." I asked them to verbalize their feelings and thoughts one sentence at a time. Once we had verbally edited their sentence, they were asked to write the sentence on paper. This deliberate process appeared to decrease their negative feelings regarding writing and gave them the confidence and freedom to edit their words. It is as though writing on paper represented permanence oral language did not possess. One can easily alter verbalizations over that of written words. In addition, many of my clients presented grave difficulty with fine-motor skills, physically grasping the pencil, writing neatly, and spelling. Hence, writing on paper represented a laborious task requiring a good portion of time.

I wanted my clients to feel unencumbered when writing, so we would often write a few sentences, erase some, or throw the whole paper away! This freedom offered them control of the writing process and the notion that alterations can be made without repercussion. Over time, my clients became capable of writing a paragraph independently when given a written prompt. For example, I might have written on the paper (for a younger client): "Please write about your favorite pet. What types of feelings do you have for this animal and why?" For a more mature client, I may have written, "Please write about your feelings regarding the events of 9/11. What types of changes have you seen occur because of this event?"

Once a certain level of independence was accomplished within their writing abilities, clients were capable of writing longer passages with less effort. Clients expressed pride regarding their writing skills, once they learned to verbalize main ideas and pertinent supporting details. We spent a great deal of time drawing conclusions, inferencing, predicting, analyzing, and evaluating. These higher order thinking skills slowly began to transfer onto paper.

Although I witnessed improvement in writing skills, I admit that not all of my clients developed an innate joy for writing (a vast majority still perceived writing to be a requirement and not an elective activity). Regardless, I believe the writing process to be fundamental in developing a foundation for critical thinking skills.

One additional suggestion for young (or reluctant writers) might be to offer photos of social scenes as a "writing prompt". When creating stories during the Mixed Bag of Emotions task in the previous chapter, the next step would be to write the story on paper. The bulk of the work will have been completed verbally with the task of producing the story in written form remaining. The creation of these stories may prove entertaining and engaging, as creative expression knows no limits!

Steps for Expressive Writing Development:

1) Ask client to verbalize thoughts and feelings one sentence at a time.

2) Edit their sentence verbally and then transfer to paper.

3) Write, erase, and throw away written work. Allow client to "own" writing process retaining control of their written work overcoming trepidation regarding perceived permanence of writing.

4) Give a written or pictorial prompt. Build upon their quality and quantity of writing over time. Main goal: ***GET THEM WRITING!***

5) Ask critical thinking skills throughout writing process.

Additional Writing Prompts

- Journal daily social experiences
- How to change a habit (good or bad)
- Feelings of stress, anger, anxiety, frustration, happiness, etc. involving an issue with their family or friends
- Personal goals
- Dreams for the future
- If they could change one thing in the world, what would it be?
- What do they love about themselves? What do they love about others?
- Their greatest fear
- Their happiest moment
- Their favorite place and why
- Their dream vacation
- If they were stuck on an island and could take one person, who would it be and why?
- Who are the most important people in your life and why?
- Their personal hero and why?
- A letter to Santa, Easter Bunny, Tooth Fairy
- A story about their first day of school

Group and Family Format

Ask the family or group to begin brainstorming and verbalize thoughts and feelings regarding a particular prompt. Use group members to flush out ideas and expressive verbalizations. Take notes while group discusses attending to the "main themes" of the discussion, or areas requiring greater detail or verbal expression. Ask members to verbalize their thoughts in a "Round Robin" fashion – allowing all group members an opportunity to verbalize.

Teach the family or group to verbalize and write main idea sentences through modeling. Illustrate the difference between main idea and detail sentences. Ask the group to practice verbalizing these types of sentences before writing them.

Ask the family or group to begin writing their ideas pertaining to the verbal discussion of the prompt. Allow 10 to 15 minutes of writing time.

Continue to build upon oral expression and writing skills until the group shows a heightened level of comfort when asked to write down their thoughts independently. Offer individualized instruction to individuals requiring further development of these skills. This may need to occur outside of the group session facilitating maximum skill development.

Part Four:

Bringing it All Together and the Family Too!

~17~
Family Education and Homework

Feelings of worth can flourish only in an atmosphere where individual differences are appreciated, mistakes are tolerated, communication is open, and rules are flexible -- the kind of atmosphere that is found in a nurturing family.
(Virginia Satir, 1916-1988)

In my personal and professional opinion, the most vital skill for humans is the ability to get along with one's family (and friends). Yes, I said it "Get along with one's family!" When I use the term "family," it represents those within the immediate core family living under one roof, extended family members who pop in for an occasional visit, or close personal friends.

I do not hold an idealistic belief that all family members must hold hands and gaze at one another lovingly. Instead, I believe families should be capable of interacting with one another in a positive and civilized manner. Families are complex human systems involving a great deal of emotional and political maneuverings more thorny than those found within the U.S. government. I myself am from the infamous "divorced family unit" and was raised by four parents. Therefore, I have a strong understanding of the politics, rules, and chains of command that can occur when four adults raise two children.

Regardless of these circumstances, one might imagine the complexity of social and emotional information within a family such as this. Personally, I believe my family educated me for my current profession; however, that is another book entirely. The point to be made with much humor is that families, no matter how they are structured, and regardless of the number of participants, are complicated human systems fascinating the fields of psychology and counseling for decades.

I do not profess to specialize in family counseling. However, a significant portion of my job includes the encouragement of a competently established family unit functioning like a well-oiled machine. After all, how can one promote effective social and emotional development only to return the child to a socially maladaptive environment not conducive to positive change?

Virginia Satir's quote at the beginning of this chapter verbalizes this notion and strikes a harmonious chord within my experiences as a counselor. In order to promote positive change within a person, they must be surrounded by an environment encouraging the flexibility required for such change. Rigid, over-bearing, dysfunctional, and/or power-hungry family environments squelch attempts for personal growth. Therefore, if the family unit demonstrates grave dysfunction, family therapy may be necessary to develop an open, tolerant, and flexible environment receptive to social development.

Family involvement within the therapeutic intervention remains essential throughout the process. The therapist should communicate and educate parents on the goals and desires of the intervention and ascertain *their goals and desires* for treatment. Both parties should agree upon the ultimate goals of therapy to avoid miscommunication regarding the desires for treatment. Written contracts, goal setting, worksheets, and illustrations (indicating techniques used, credentials of therapist, and implementation of therapeutic tools) are helpful methods assuring informed consent has been sufficiently addressed.

Boosting the Mind's Eye is a family endeavor because the client relies upon support and interaction with their family to successfully complete the designated tasks. The work within this program will not fall solely upon the targeted client, as the family is asked to image and verbalize social and emotional information as well.

Because the family constitutes the core of the client's daily environment, the family environment will serve as "homework" to engage in newly learned social and emotional skills. The client's application of skills may occur directly due to an assignment given by the therapist, or simply as a natural application of the client's newly developed skills. Therefore, recruit the family's direct involvement through education and therapeutic intervention.

Getting Down to Business

I encourage several methods of familial intervention. In the past, my session times ran between 90 to 120 minutes. This allowed for both individual and family interventions to occur. I would treat the client individually by providing a combination of learning and psychotherapy intervention and then ask the parent(s) to attend the last 20-30 minutes of the session time. Family counseling offered an opportunity to focus upon communication within the family, family roles, parental input, question and answer sessions, parent education, and a myriad of other services necessitated by the family. My primary therapeutic responsibility rested with the child and their individual intervention; therefore, my intervention with the family was primarily offering support and education.

Presently, I suggest a more direct therapeutic familial approach using the steps of this program. The family should be offered therapeutic time to learn and engage within the tasks. Currently, I offer *Boosting the Mind's Eye* in a group format with 3 to 4 individuals per group (grouped according to age). I meet with the group once weekly for 90 minutes, at which time we engage within the tasks previously described. Every three sessions, I ask the family members to join the group for the last half of the session time.

During this time, I teach the programs steps to the families and ask the group members to interact with their families demonstrating role-play techniques, describing photos, engaging in vocabulary acquisition, social stories, etc... Group members are encouraged to "teach" their families the processes and techniques learned to empower and increase self-confidence.

The family sessions are an appropriate time to use visualization exercises, or role-playing as it pertains to specific situations at home. What better way to reinforce a concept than to use personal and emotional experiences occurring within the family unit? In addition to group members working with their own families, it is often helpful to mix up the families and have them work with one another. This process builds rapport and friendship across the families, as they tend to share common emotional and social experiences. Families offer one another support as they identify with the difficulties of raising children, as well as children with social and emotional deficits.

Whether you choose to create a group setting for family work, or merely work with individual clients and their families, the overall goal remains to buffer emotional and social skills within the family by applying the steps of the program. Derailing (focus of therapy getting 'off track') occurs often in family therapy, as many personalities are present in the room. However, derailing may be reduced through preset goals, organization of the session, and firm communication boundaries.

I often begin an initial family session by verbalizing the goals of the session, as well as any "rules" of communication that should transpire (i.e. not interrupting one another, respectful listening, reframing techniques, body language, etc…). Powerful emotions and social issues may arise and be addressed by processing the emotions and visualizing a preferred outcome.

Over time, I have discovered that my style of therapeutic intervention is goal-oriented and focused upon developing abilities and processes within the brain. I feel it is vital for families to perceive progress and witness this within the behavioral and emotional displays of the family members. I believe that emotional and social intelligence can be improved upon with didactic and experiential interventions.

In order to end the session in a timely fashion, I offer the family a 5-minute warning allowing wind down time and closure of the session. I summarize the contents of the session while positively reinforcing the efforts of each family member. Encouragement is a powerful reinforcer for families working to improve upon their skills. Developing new skills and revamping old habits is no easy task; therefore, positively reinforcing small steps in the right direction offers an individual the support and guidance needed to motivate their commitment to the process.

Many a day, I have given my families the 5-minute warning before closing the session and an enormous "emotional bomb" was dropped by one of the family members. The inclination of an eager and helpful therapist (speaking from professional experience) would be to dig in and begin working on the issue. As long as no individual is at risk of harming themselves, or another (if so, it would be necessary to go into "crises mode" taking the necessary steps to ensure physical safety), I tend to consistently model the importance of maintaining the time boundaries of the session. Therefore, in this situation, I may state:

> "That sounds like an extremely important issue we should address. However, our time today does not allow for it. So, I am going to write this down to be sure we discuss this issue at the *very beginning* of our

next session giving it the time it deserves. As a good rule of thumb, if you have a really important issue you would like to discuss, please bring it up at the beginning of the session to ensure it gets the time and attention it deserves."

This statement helps set the tone for the flow of session time demonstrating that therapy has a beginning, middle, and end. Without consistent rhythm to the sessions (especially when working with groups or families), chaos may ensue and individuals feel as though their ideas were not given adequate time. Time is of the essence and when developing skills using specific techniques, setting the pace and tone of the session is helpful.

I do not wish to imply rigidity; but merely structure with flexibility. Being flexible is a vital component of therapy; however, it does not denote disorganized chaos. As a therapist, you will find your own ebb and flow setting the rhythm of your therapy sessions. Once this balance has been struck, the sessions will pace smoothly allowing for a comfortable working relationship.

Suggestions for Family Work

- Allot specific and consistent time for family intervention.

- Create a family therapy plan matching the progress and skills of your individual client.

- Discuss learned and practiced skills during family sessions.

- Ask parents to read coinciding chapters involved in their child's treatment of *Boosting the Mind's Eye*.

- Give family specific homework bolstering treatment (i.e. vocabulary words, writing prompts, family photos to describe, role play exercises)

- Set boundaries for communication and model appropriate expression of feelings (such as, 'I feel…' statements).

- Practice role-playing, vocabulary building, and imagery exercises during family sessions.

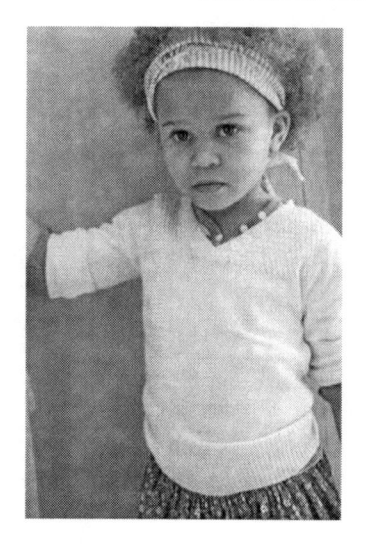

~18~
Family Role Play

Working with children has been one of the most gratifying experiences in my life akin to having my own. Children are filled with energy offering hope to society's future. I take pleasure in listening to their stories and dreams, as their view of the world is often colored with innocent wonder. Assisting a child with cognitive and emotional development reaps the rewards of witnessing transformation within a child's abilities resulting in a renewed sense of self-confidence. A happy child often requires no further explanation.

The portion of my job creating the greatest challenge is – believe it or not – the involvement of the family. Family intervention is both rewarding and effective; however, a great deal more challenging. Parents possess strong feelings regarding the rearing and education of their children – *as they well should!* Strong emotions may cloud a parent's perception of their own behavior, or their child's, within the family unit.

I believe in the transformation of human behavior made possible through a didactic forum. Information can be transferred using a myriad of interesting methods. Incorporating auditory (hearing), haptic (touch), and visual (imagery) teaching methods allows for a greater multitude of people to learn and understand. Learning styles are different across populations and cultures; therefore, I believe that an assortment of teaching techniques should be utilized. This idea rests upon the notion that not all therapy is "talk therapy."

The family's involvement remains paramount in the acquisition and retention of social and emotional information not only for the client, but for the entire family. By introducing the family to the social and emotional concepts discussed throughout this book, one may create an atmosphere of positive change.

The following sample dialogue demonstrates a family role-playing and switching roles fostering empathy and understanding regarding one another's role within the family. The overall goal remains to improve communication skills and emotional connectedness.

Sample Dialogue: (Therapist and family of four – Mom, Dad, son, Zane (13 years), and daughter, Kate (the identified client, 9 years).

Therapist:	"We have discussed some of the skills you'd like to improve upon in the family. I have heard several of you say that you think others in the family don't understand how you feel. I wonder if we can try a role-playing exercise allowing you to switch roles with one another. This will help to understand how it might feel to be a different person in your own family. The first "switches" I'd like to see are Mom and Dad switching roles and Zane and Kate switching roles. I want to create a setting for our role-play. So, I want everyone to imagine a day at the park. Picture a nice picnic lunch on the green grass with a pretty blue sky and a cool breeze

blowing. This is going to be the setting for your "family meeting" where you decide something together as a family. Does everyone have their park pictured in their head? (Family nods approval). Great! Now, I want you to discuss and decide upon a family vacation. You can choose anywhere you want to go, but you have to discuss your opinion based upon the person you are enacting in the family. So, you have to speak and give opinions as you believe the person you are playing would. Does everyone understand?"

Kate: "So, you want me to talk as if I'm Zane and bring up ideas that I think he would like?"

Therapist: "That is exactly right, Kate, you've got it. Are you ready to begin? Ok, let's hear your discussion."

Dad: (as Mom)
"Well, I would like to go to a nice sandy beach, so I can relax. We have such hectic lives that it would be nice to go someplace peaceful."

Mom: (as Dad)
"That's nice, but I'd like to go to a theme park somewhere, like Disney World. That way, the kids can enjoy the park and maybe I can play some golf."

Zane: (as Kate)
"I think we should go skiing. We've never gone before and I think it would be fun to learn how."

Kate: (as Zane)
"Do we have to go anywhere? I would rather hang out with my friends than go on some family vacation!"

Therapist:
"You all are doing great. I like how everyone has a different opinion about where they'd like to go. Now, start negotiating with one another in order to make a decision about where you might actually go. How will you decide upon your trip so that a compromise is reached?

Mom: (as Dad)
"Well, I think that since I'm the Dad, I should get to decide because I am paying for the whole thing."

Dad: (as Mom)
"That's ridiculous! Just because you're the breadwinner, doesn't mean you get to make all of the decisions. I think we need to figure out a fair way to let everyone decide."

Kate: (as Zane)
"Why doesn't everyone write down their idea and put it in a hat and then let one person draw? Whatever is drawn is where go as a family. That way nobody has really chosen, it's all up to the draw!"

Zane: (as Kate)
"Ok, but I want to draw because I never get to do anything."

Mom: (as Dad)
"I think that is a great idea and I would be

willing to go along with that if your mother agrees."

Dad: (as Mom)
"I think that sounds fair. But, I will only agree if everyone promises not to whine or pout about what is picked. Whatever we do, it will be as one big happy family. Agreed?"

The Family: "Agreed!"

The family writes down their choices and puts them into Zane's baseball hat. Zane draws (as he is acting as Kate) and reads the answer.

Zane: (as Kate)
"Well, it looks like we're going to Disney World!"

Mom: (as Dad)
"Yippee! I've always wanted to meet Mickey Mouse!"

Dad: (as Mom)
"I think this is a great choice because everyone in the family will be able to find something they enjoy. I am looking forward to having fun with you guys!"

Therapist: "I couldn't have created a better scenario. You guys negotiated that like pros! Great job – all of you! Let's talk about how it felt to play one another in the family."

Mom: "I had to think about how my husband would respond to things before I spoke. It made me realize his role and how he views

>   the family. I liked that because I can understand his perspective."

Dad: "It made me realize how invested my wife is in the emotional parts of the family. She is always the caring one spending time ensuring everyone is happy and feels good about what we do. It was nice to play that role and made me realize that I can do more of that as a Dad in this family."

Kate: "I liked being Zane because he is older and has more say-so in the family. Plus, it was fun acting older and knowing that people may listen to you more."

Zane: "I liked being Kate because she's the baby in the family. Sometimes I think she gets away with more because she's younger. But, it is not always fun to be the baby because people don't listen to you as much. This was pretty fun."

Therapist: "You guys did a great job. I can't wait for next week's role playing scenario. I will have to think of a something creative to challenge you all!"

~19~
Multi-Cultural Considerations

My desire to add this chapter into the book remains twofold: 1) I believe that as humans, both personally and professionally, we should improve upon our acceptance of multi-cultural differences. 2) I believe this program may benefit those desiring to improve upon their imagery abilities; however, the foundational concepts of this book may be culturally skewed.

Prior to writing this book, I made the grave assumption that all people wish to improve upon their social and emotional skills. However, being capable of expressing one's self clearly, directly, and succinctly are not necessarily attributes all people desire. My hope is that individuals can use the techniques within this book and tailor their own social desires and needs to the actual techniques themselves. In addition, as cultural differences may dictate alternative communication styles, the idea that visual imagery can bolster all language will hopefully transcend across varying cultures.

Our Way or the Highway

Therapists, educators, parents, professionals, or for that matter, any inhabitant of the world should consider multi-cultural differences. The textbook, *Counseling the Culturally Diverse*, presents the argument that multi-cultural considerations should be taken into account for all professionals within the fields of counseling and psychology.[1] I will amend this by stating that *all people* should consider differences amongst cultures when forming opinions. Understanding the divergence across cultural communities aids our ability to form educated and valid opinions versus using stereotypes and prejudicial thinking to create rash judgments.

The fields of counseling and psychology in this country were not founded upon multi-cultural distinctions. Most therapeutic interventions applied in the U.S. are based upon Euro-American, or White middle to upper-class values, such as individualism, autonomy, and responsibility.[1] Surprisingly, these values are not always considered the "norm" throughout the world. The Euro-American value of personal independence is not necessarily valued across collective cultures and may create bias, especially in the therapy room.[1] Therefore, one must consider culture and background when attending to a client's needs. To assure greater sensitivity regarding multicultural distinctions, therapists should reflect upon their own values and biases, including any stereotypes they may possess. Through reflection and education, professionals may create an open and flexible outlook allowing greater cultural understanding.

Stigmas and Stereotypes

Individuals in stigmatized "master status" groups (i.e. women, poor, gay, Black, Asian-American, Latino) are perceived to lack many of the characteristics White culture views as positive.[2] Stigmatized groups are often not viewed to be "independent, unemotional, objective, dominant, active, competitive, logical, adventurous, or direct," which are considered positive personal attributes by the White culture. Members of stigmatized master status groups may be viewed as "problems, immoral, and disease-ridden," serving to dismiss any claims of discrimination made by the minority.[2]

If the professional perception exists that the "other" is at fault because it is their "nature," or part of their genetic make-up, then we as professionals are to blame. Helping professionals must be capable of shifting the focus of the problem from stigmatized clients onto themselves to achieve greater self-awareness.[1]

Additionally, if therapists continually overlook the values within a person's group membership, stigmatization of minority groups perpetuates.[1] Mere good intention, knowledge, and "color-blindness" are not sufficient when providing multi-cultural counseling. One cannot presuppose clinical interventions to be value-free capable of exerting positive change for all client populations. If we continue to behave as no differences exist between people, we are creating as much damage as harping on the differences themselves. We must increase our awareness and change our therapeutic behavior accordingly.

Clinical Considerations

The mental health field has been criticized for the imposition of White-middle class ideals onto the client (such as individualism, autonomy, and responsibility).[1] Therapists may attempt to draw these characteristics out of their clients creating "optimal mental health" without regarding whether the client's cultural values truly embrace these changes.

If an individual does not achieve the therapeutic goals, they may be blamed for their lack of success and viewed as a failure. This "blaming the victim" scenario ignores outside influences, such as bias, discrimination, and prejudice, acting as the real culprit blocking an individual's personal success and happiness. In other words, individuals belonging to a stigmatized group may often be attempting to survive day-to-day. They may not have the resources or time to concern themselves with empathy and insight. Their life may include issues concerning food, safety, shelter, and employment. As therapists, it is our job to attend to their needs without presupposing our values and desires for "proper clinical intervention." Therefore, our job may include more than one therapeutic hat. We may find ourselves including vocational counseling, advice-giving, or social work into our repertoire of services.

Advice-giving and disclosure are not fundamental to the Euro-American style of therapy, as we are trained to reflect, provide insight, and redirect a person's thoughts and behaviors.[1] However, other cultures may perceive this indirect verbal communication lacking involvement and caring on the part of the therapist. Hence, advice-giving can may be necessary and warranted dependent upon the needs of the client.

Power Differential

In an interview with Dr. Beverly Greene, a professor at St. John's University in New York City, regarding power and diversity issues, she discussed a valid point regarding the choices people make when examining differences amongst humans. She noted that we *choose* to look at the characteristic differences of ethno-racial identity, biological sex, gender roles, age, disability, and sexual orientation when comparing individuals.[3]

She perceived these differences to be important to us because they are based upon power differentials occurring amongst these groups. In other words, these differences are focused upon because they maintain the status quo and power hierarchy within our society. However, she noted that we never discuss the *actual power differentials* amongst these groups as a characteristic difference between groups, which is the vital component when addressing diversity issues. We spend a great deal of time and money conducting studies, interviews, census measures; and yet, we never stop to ask ourselves *why* we need to know these differences.

Does merely knowing the differences amongst groups aid us in the ability to become less biased? Or, does it give us additional characteristics to label groups forming a greater expanse across people?

When considering power differentials occurring within the therapy room, one should consider their own need for power within a therapeutic relationship. Maintaining the "authority and expert" status tips the power balance in the therapist's favor, which may impede the course of therapy. As mentioned previously, one method creating positive rapport and trust with younger clients is to tip the power scale in their favor by taking a "one-down" position. As therapists, we are often trained to be the "expert;" however, this frame of reference may impede therapeutic rapport and progress.

Take Away Message

The inclusion of this chapter reveals the unattractive truth regarding our society and issues of discrimination and bias. I believe it is a worthy soap box to stand upon, as our country continues to grow and change daily regarding multicultural differences. Growing up on the border of Mexico offered a perspective many within the White culture will never have the opportunity to comprehend. Learning a new language, culture, and style of communication allowed a personal sense of flexibility and malleability seldom required of an individual within the majority White culture.

Because of my exposure and identification as a minority status throughout my childhood and adolescence, I empathize with the struggles stigmatized groups often experience. Both Brownsville and Laredo, Texas were 98-99% Hispanic at that time. Therefore, being blonde-haired, blue-eyed, and very pale skinned tended to draw attention. I learned very young that being "different" was not necessarily admirable, but required an ability to shift one's thinking and behaviors to be socially accepted.

Is my transformation and acculturation as a youth similar to the changes we ask individuals who are not White, heterosexual, and middle class to achieve in the U.S.? Media portrays White middle-class, heterosexual America to be the "norm" for which others should embrace and therefore, alter themselves to become, lest they receive social rejection.

As we become more "politically correct" in our jargon and media, we tend to maintain the misperception that discrimination and bias do not exist as they once did 50 to 100 years ago. Maybe we have become reticent in our attempts to evolve into a more culturally aware and diverse country. Although America prides itself on the "melting pot" concept of race and culture, one may perceive America to be more of a "tossed salad" with divergent races and cultures maintaining their own sets of values and beliefs whilst living amongst one another.

The issues of discrimination and bigotry are still very much alive. Whether it is racism, class-ism, age-ism, sexual orientation-ism, gender-ism, religion-ism; we live in a time when judgment and criticism are rendered unfairly to stigmatized minority groups. These issues should create concern if we desire positive social outcomes for the future generations of America.

~20~
Wrappin' it Up!

If by now, I have not qualified under the term "redundant," I will at this moment. The gist of this program remains to bolster an individual's visual imagery allowing the visual part of the brain to aid in the comprehension and retention of social and emotional information. This book is created for the purposes of adding to one's "tool belt," by boosting imaging abilities, as well as social and emotional intelligence.

I do not confess this to be the paramount program to which all should subscribe. I find that to be narcissistic and utterly impossible. Reinventing the wheel within any field can often be a difficult task. Therefore, in lieu of breaking entirely new ground, I have put several "wheels" together creating, perhaps, a motorized vehicle of sorts. The combined ideas behind Dual Coding Theory and the Four-Branch Model of Emotional Intelligence highlight the importance of developing and utilizing imagery for social and emotional abilities outside traditional educational and therapeutic models.

Over-Active Imagination

No one would be harmed by enhancing their visualization abilities. Even individuals blessed with above average visualization may polish their skills by performing some of the aforementioned tasks. To exemplify this concept, I will relay a personal story. While attending Southern Methodist University earning my Master's in Clinical/Counseling Psychology, I was simultaneously working for a Lindamood-Bell® clinic in Dallas.

While working at this clinic, I was trained in learning modalities aiding those with learning disorders to read, write, spell, and comprehend. However, whilst administering the techniques associated with the Visualizing and Verbalizing® program, I noticed a vast difference in my own study habits. I found myself reading the material what I termed "more deeply," which meant that I seemed to read a bit more slowly, but retained far more information. I no longer required hours of study, or study aids to perform well on my exams.

In his book, *Opening the Mind's Eye*, Ian Robertson describes individuals who are visual learners versus verbal learners. He stated that visual learners often take longer to read because they are creating more imagery within the mind's eye.[1] I realized that my exposure to teaching visual techniques heightened my own imaging abilities, decreasing my need to study, and still maintaining good grades during graduate school.

One does not necessarily need to possess weakness within their imagery system to benefit from imagery exercises. Bodybuilders who are in "perfect" shape are usually not harmed by an additional workout; instead these extra hours in the gym typically add to and maintain their stellar physique. Similarly, our minds may benefit from a "tune up" of sorts maintaining and/or improving upon existing abilities.

As a parent or professional administering this program, you may find yourself creating more vivid images over the course of time. This is a great side effect of administering visual techniques.

Digressing with a personal anecdote, I had one of these

"over-active imagination moments" recently while visiting the chiropractor. I attend the chiropractor regularly and perform physical therapy exercises involving head weights that are wrapped around my head. While demonstrating how to use my head weights, the chiropractor, who was wearing a bright green shirt and has a shaved head, lifted two small rectangular head weights up to his head where horns might grow. I immediately began to giggle, which of course, made the good Dr. a bit uneasy. I could not control the vivid image that popped into my mind while he held these two weights up like horns. Wearing a bright green shirt and with a bald head – he looked a bit like Shrek (obviously I had watched this one too many times with my daughters). I tried to explain my image to him, which he took some humor in (I think, or thought I was calling him an ogre from the swamp); however, this serves as a silly example of how one's imagination can run a bit wild. Prior to tapping into my visual imagery daily for work, I had lost that sense of imagination children often possess.

Adults may term the imagination of children as "over-active;" however, I would offer that they are not *over-active*, but merely *more active* than an adult's imagination. Maybe as adults, it is our imagination that is too limited. I find it humorous that adults need to quantify what is *too much* or *too little* for children when what is considered excessive, or insufficient to us, works perfectly well for them.

Why not live in a world where fairies and green monsters hang out in your room? I suppose because as an adult, we would term this type of experience a hallucination and seek immediate psychiatric help. However, I would offer that adults might benefit from a healthy dose of an "over-active" imagination - if not to create a little spark within our lives, to add humor and fun to an otherwise busy and demanding day.

Live a Little, Laugh a Lot, and Live a Lot Longer!
I firmly believe that adding humor and light-heartedness to daily life offers potential for positive change. Being capable of laughing at life's follies creates room for joy where stress and sadness may otherwise reside. To exemplify, allow me to paint a silly scenario. Imagine that you are fighting with a loved one, be it a spouse or a family member. Words and emotions were flying through the air at a loud and alarming pace. Then, out of no where, your family dog lying on the ground looking utterly bored passes gas. You pause, look at the dog, and begin to laugh hysterically. The fight has left you as laughter and humor have taken its place.

Okay, maybe this only happens in my house, but the concept behind this story remains sound. During moments of high tension and stress, humorous distraction breaks the dissonant chord of anger by bestowing the harmonious chord of humor. Imagine it as a little fairy sprinkling "happy dust" on the situation by creating room for laughter where there might otherwise be tears.

In his book, *Social Intelligence*, Daniel Goleman offers research stating that couples mirror one another's body language, mood, and physiological arousal. Therefore, as one shifts into a high gear of anger, the other follows suit.[2] Imagine your most recent emotionally charged argument. Recall the physical sensations during and after this harrowing event. Was your breathing and heart rate elevated? Did you clench your jaw, tighten your shoulders, and curl your fists into a ball? Did you feel as though you wanted to physically fight, or had just finished one?

If we were capable of instilling more humor into daily interactions, wouldn't life seem less stressful? Maybe this sounds simplistic and a far-fetched, but I assure you that even the smallest amounts of infused joviality into daily life reaps the benefits of a fuller, healthier existence. It has been found in a study conducted at the Indiana State University Sycamore Nursing Center that laughter reduces stress and improves the activity of natural killer cells. This research has implications for cancer patients, as laughter may improve their ability to survive cancer.[3] Who could have imagined gaiety increasing an individual's probability of surviving one the most feared human diseases?

Utilize imagery as a medium to explore your humor more fully by picturing funny scenes when you feel yourself becoming agitated and angry. Verbalize these humorous images to your spouse or loved ones to ease the tension of a hairy situation. If you find yourselves arguing with an individual, imagine them with a baby bonnet and pacifier in order to perceive them as more innocent and child-like.

Bottom-line: Use imagery to infuse laughter and happiness within your life! Whether through the steps of *Boosting the Mind's Eye* fostering social and emotional intelligence, or becoming an improved bed-time story teller, imagery offers all individuals the opportunity to improve upon their present abilities. I believe all individuals possess the capability of using their mind's eye to brighten their lives. Now, all you have to do is simply ***IMAGINE*** the possibilities!

Appendix 1:
Emotional Vocabulary Index

A

Accentuate
Accountable
Accuse
Adamant
Admittance
Affection
Affectionate
Afraid
Aggravate
Aggression
Aggressive
Alarmed
Alliance
Amaze
Amuse
Angry
Angst
Anguish
Annoyed
Anticipate
Anxiety
Anxious
Apathetic
Apologetic
Appreciation
Apprehension
Argumentative
Arrogant
Ashamed
Assemble
Assertive
Asset
Astonish
Attribute
Awe
Awkward

B

Bashful
Behavior
Believing
Bereavement
Bewildered
Bitter
Blame
Blissful
Blue
Boastful
Body language
Bold
Bored
Boundaries
Brash
Brave

C

Cackle
Caddy
Calm
Caring
Cautious
Chaos
Cheerful
Cold
Commitment
Commotion
Compliant
Concentrate
Concern

Condemn
Confidence
Confident
Confront
Confusion
Content
Converge
Corny
Courage
Cowardice
Coy
Criticize
Cunning
Curious

Dishonesty
Dislike
Dismay
Disorder
Disorientation
Dissatisfy
Distasteful
Distract
Distress
Disturb
Drained
Dread
Drowsy
Doubtful

D

Daring
Deceive
Decisive
Defeated
Defy
Delighted
Denial
Depressed
Depression
Depth
Desperate
Despondent
Determined
Disappointed
Disapprove
Disbelieve
Discipline
Discontent
Discourage
Disgust

E

Eager
Ecstatic
Elated
Embarrassed
Emotional
Empathy
Emphasis
Endure
Enraged
Enthusiastic
Envious
Exasperated
Excitement
Exclude
Exhaustion
Exhilarate
Expectant
Expression

F

Facial Expressions
Failure
Faith
Family
Fascinated
Fatigue
Fault
Fear
Fearless
Fervent
Flexible
Focus
Fondness
Forgetful
Forced
Forward
Forte
Fretful
Friendship
Frightened
Frustration
Fun-loving
Furious

G

Genial
Giddy
Glad
Gleeful
Gloomy
Goaded
Gossip
Grateful
Gratitude
Greedy
Gregarious
Grief
Grieving
Grimace
Grossed out
Guidance
Guilt

H

Hackneyed
Happy
Hassle
Hate
Headstrong
Heartache
Helpful
Helpless
Heroic
Hesitate
Honest
Hope
Horrify
Hot
Humiliate
Humor
Hurt

I

Ignore
Ill
Imagery
Imagine

Immature
Impatience
Importance
Impossible
Impress
Include
Indifferent
Inflexible
Inhibited
Innocent
Insane
Insecure
Insensitive
Inspire
Integrity
Intensity
Interest
Interfere
Interrogate
Introvert
Irritation

J

Jaded
Jealous
Jolly
Jostling
Journaling
Jovial
Joyful
Judgment
Juvenile

K

Kind

L

Language
Lazy
Lethargic
Liking
Lively
Lonely
Lovable
Love
Love struck
Loyalty

M

Manic
Marriage
Mayhem
Melancholy
Mental
Merry
Mischievous
Miserable
Misery
Mistake
Misunderstanding
Moody
Mournful
Movement
Muddle
Mysterious
Mystified

N

Nauseated
Negative
Nervous
Nightmare
Noble

O

Obligated
Obstinate
Oppositional
Optimistic
Outgoing
Overwhelmed
Overworked

P

Panic
Pained
Paralanguage
Passionate
Patience
Perplexed
Persistent
Perturbed
Physical
Phobia
Pitiful
Pleasant
Pleading
Plucky
Ponder
Positive

Potency
Power
Pressured
Prim
Proud
Provoked
Puzzled

Q

Quaint
Quiet

R

Reduce
Regretful
Rejection
Relationships
Relax
Reliability
Relieved
Remorseful
Remote
Reprimand
Reproach
Resentful
Reserved
Respect
Responsible
Role-playing

S

Sad
Safety

Satisfied
Scowl
Security
Self-assured
Self-confident
Self-conscious
Sensitive
Siblings
Sick
Silly
Sincerity
Shamed
Sheepish
Shocked
Shy
Sleepy
Smug
Solitary
Sorrowful
Sorry
Stifle
Strain
Strength
Stressed
Stubborn
Suffer
Sulky
Surprised
Surrender
Suspicious
Sweet
Sympathetic

T

Talkative
Tenacious

Tender
Tense
Tension
Terrified
Terror
Timid
Tired
Therapy
Thoughtful
Threatened
Thrilled
Tortured
Tone
Trauma
Trite
Triumphant
Truthfulness
Turmoil
Two-faced

U

Uncertain
Understanding
Unenthusiastic
Unhappiness
Unprovoked
Unrealistic
Upheaval
Urgency

V

Vain
Verbalize
Virtuous

Visualize
Vulnerable

W

Warmth
Weary
Whimsical
Willing
Withdrawn
Woe
Worried

Appendix 2:
Facial Expression Photos

Part I:

Happy
Playful

Boosting the Mind's Eye

Photo By: Steve Visneau

Boosting the Mind's Eye

Photo By: Steve Visneau

Photo By: Steve Visneau

BOOSTING THE MIND'S EYE

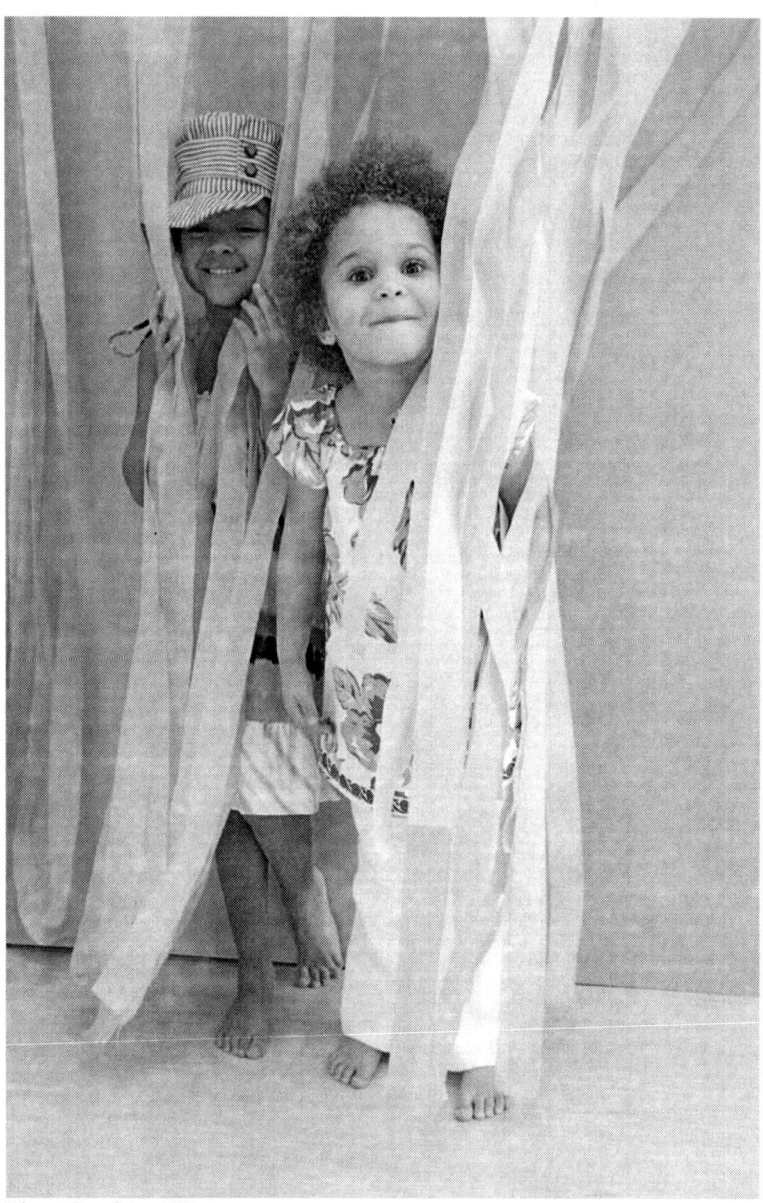

Photo By: Steve Visneau

Boosting the Mind's Eye

Photo By: Steve Visneau

Photo By: Steve Visneau

Boosting the Mind's Eye

Photo By: Steve Visneau

BOOSTING THE MIND'S EYE

Photo By: Alisha Robins Stump

Boosting the Mind's Eye

Photo By: Alisha Robins Stump

Boosting the Mind's Eye

Photo By: Alisha Robins Stump

BOOSTING THE MIND'S EYE

Photo By: Alisha Robins Stump

Photo By: Steve Visneau

Boosting the Mind's Eye

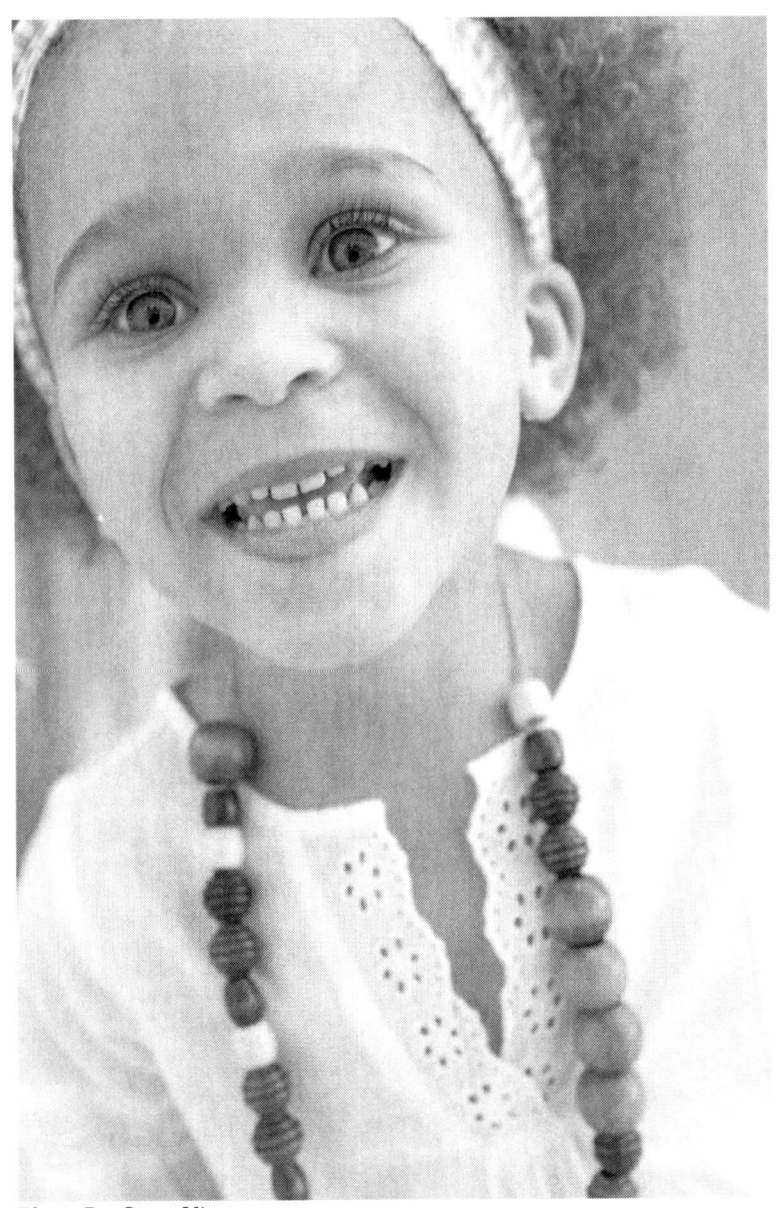

Photo By: Steve Visneau

BOOSTING THE MIND'S EYE

Photo By: Steve Visneau

BOOSTING THE MIND'S EYE

Photo By: Steve Visneau

Boosting the Mind's Eye

Photo By: Steve Visneau

Photo By: Alisha Robins Stump

Part II:

Shy
Embarrassed
Mischievous

Photo By: Steve Visneau

BOOSTING THE MIND'S EYE

Photo By: Steve Visneau

BOOSTING THE MIND'S EYE

Photo By: Steve Visneau

Photo By: Steve Visneau

Boosting the Mind's Eye

Photo By: Steve Visneau

BOOSTING THE MIND'S EYE

Photo By: Steve Visneau

BOOSTING THE MIND'S EYE

Photo By: Steve Visneau

BOOSTING THE MIND'S EYE

Photo By: Alisha Robins Stump

Photo By: Alisha Robins Stump

Photos By: Alisha Robins Stump

BOOSTING THE MIND'S EYE

Photo By: Steve Visneau

BOOSTING THE MIND'S EYE

Photo By: Steve Visneau

Part III:

Surprise
Fear
Shock

Boosting the Mind's Eye

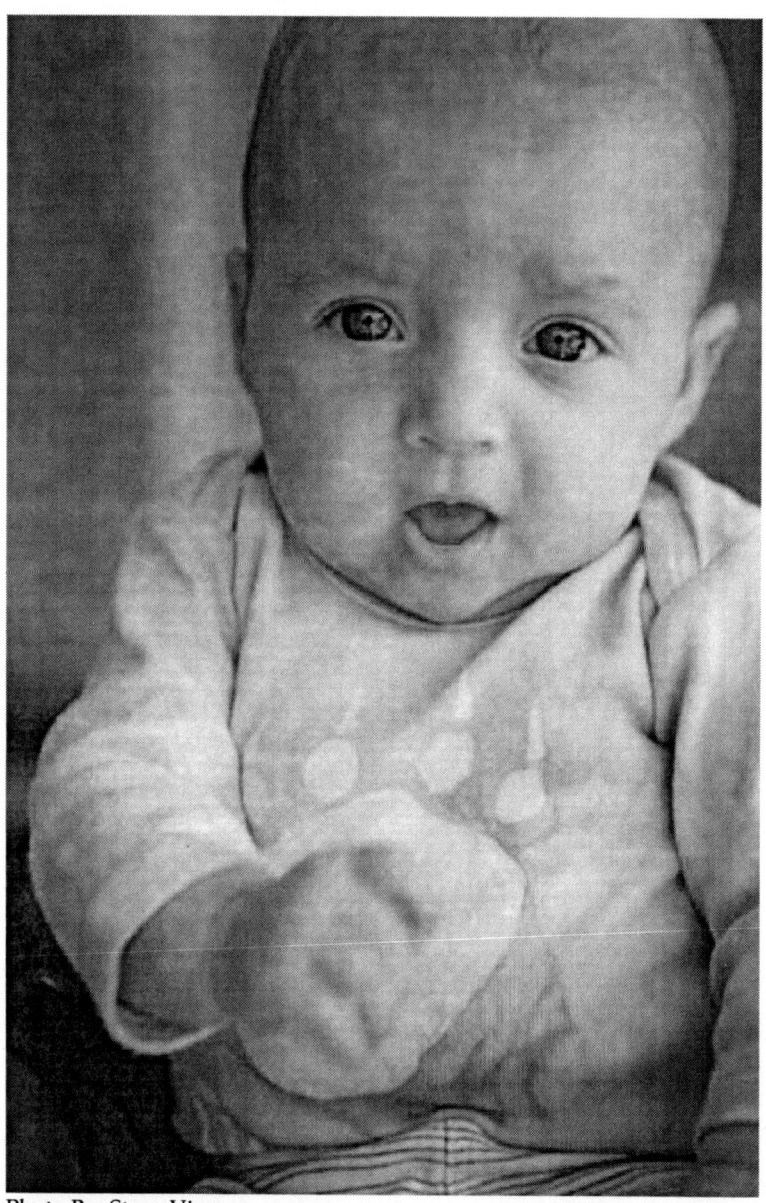

Photo By: Steve Visneau

Photo By: Steve Visneau

Boosting the Mind's Eye

Photo By: Alisha Robins Stump

BOOSTING THE MIND'S EYE

Photo By: Alisha Robins Stump

Boosting the Mind's Eye

Photo By: Alisha Robins Stump

Part IV:

Upset
Anger
Irritation
Annoyance
Frustration

BOOSTING THE MIND'S EYE

Photo By: Steve Visneau

BOOSTING THE MIND'S EYE

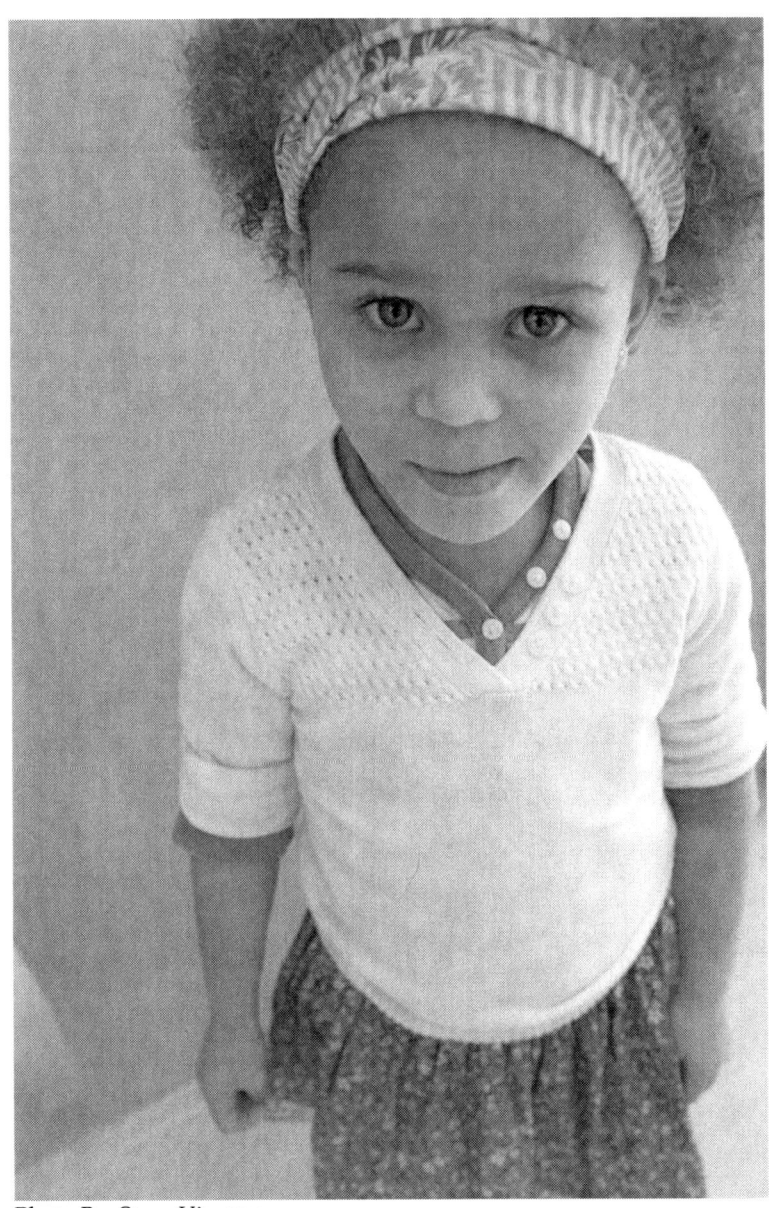

Photo By: Steve Visneau

Photo By: Alisha Robins Stump

Photo By: Alisha Robins Stump

Boosting the Mind's Eye

Photo By: Alisha Robins Stump

Boosting the Mind's Eye

Photo By: Alisha Robins Stump

Photo By: Alisha Robins Stump

Boosting the Mind's Eye

Photo By: Alisha Robins Stump

Boosting the Mind's Eye

Photo By: Alisha Robins Stump

Boosting the Mind's Eye

Photo By: Alisha Robins Stump

BOOSTING THE MIND'S EYE

Photo By: Alisha Robins Stump

Boosting the Mind's Eye

Photo By: Alisha Robins Stump

BOOSTING THE MIND'S EYE

Photo By: Steve Visneau

Part V:

Serious
Neutral
Thoughtful
Pensive

BOOSTING THE MIND'S EYE

Photo By: Alisha Robins Stump

Photo By: Alisha Robins Stump

Photo By: Alisha Robins Stump

BOOSTING THE MIND'S EYE

Photo By: Steve Visneau

Photo By: Steve Visneau

BOOSTING THE MIND'S EYE

Photo By: Steve Visneau

Photo By: Steve Visneau

Boosting the Mind's Eye

Photo By: Steve Visneau

BOOSTING THE MIND'S EYE

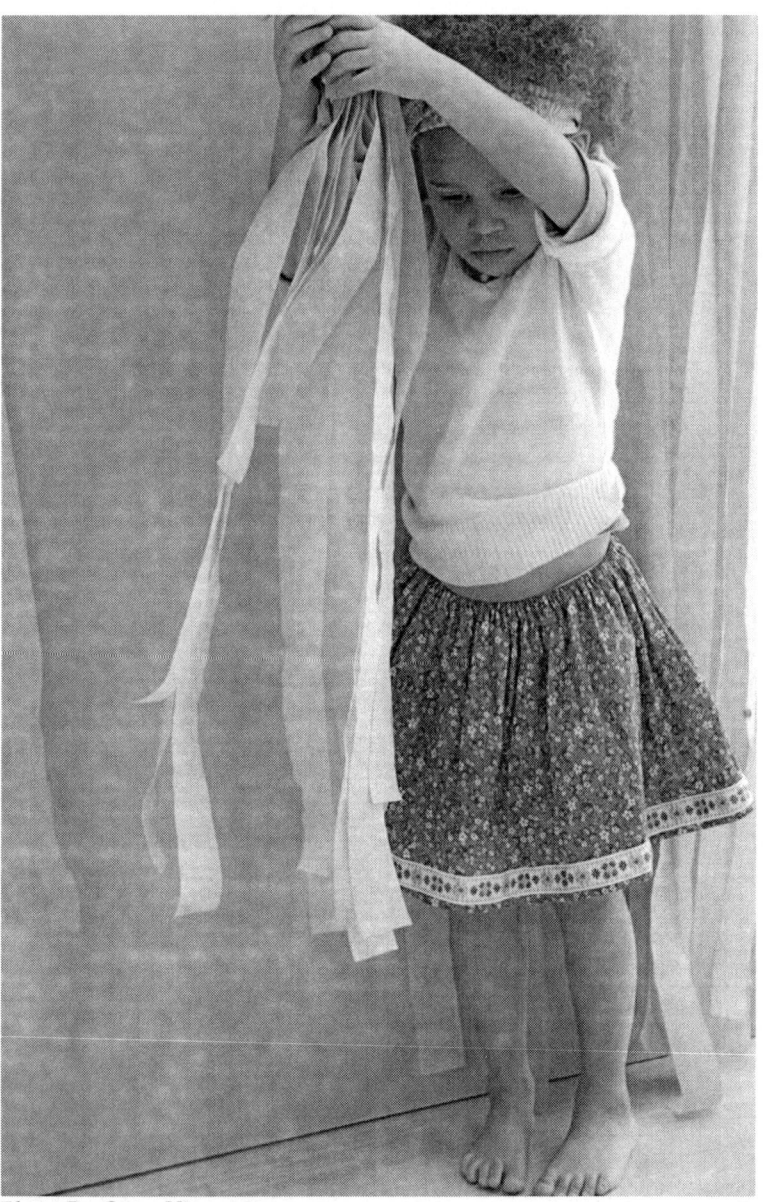

Photo By: Steve Visneau

BOOSTING THE MIND'S EYE

Photo By: Steve Visneau

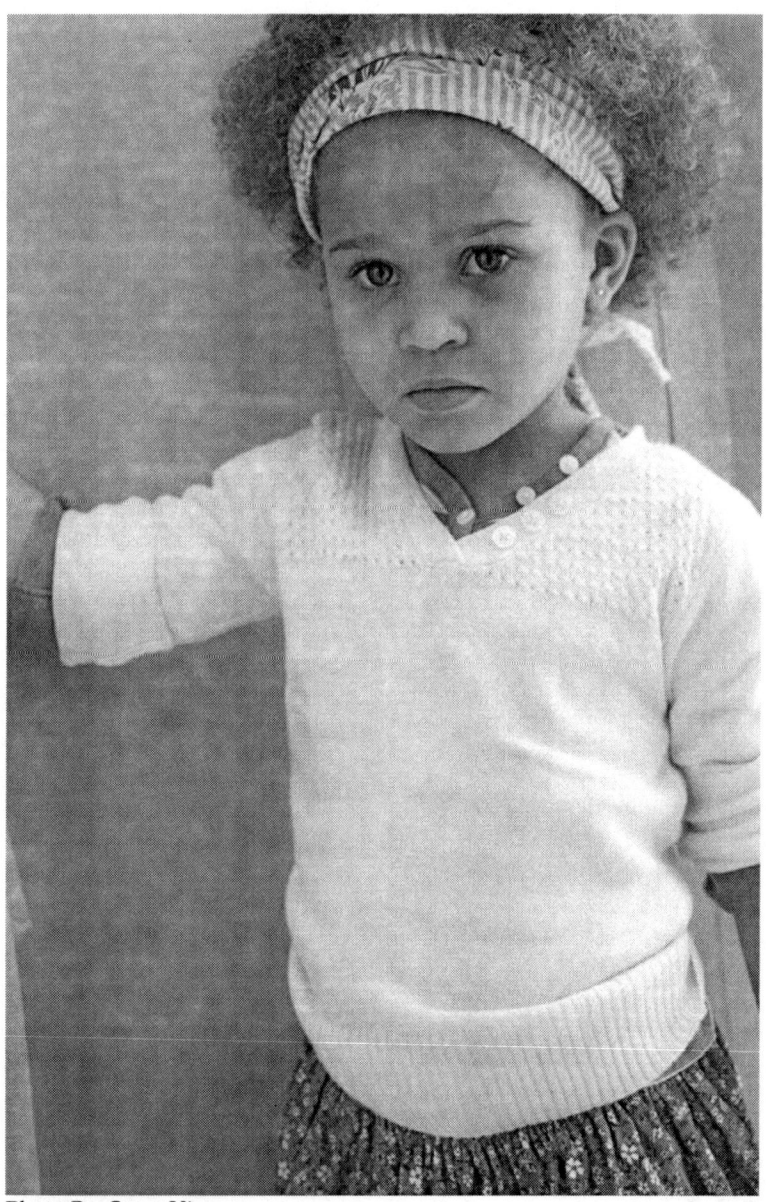

Photo By: Steve Visneau

Part VI:

Emotions Open for Interpretation

BOOSTING THE MIND'S EYE

Photo By: Alisha Robins Stump

BOOSTING THE MIND'S EYE

Photo By: Steve Visneau

Photo By: Steve Visneau

Photo By: Alisha Robins Stump

Photo By: Alisha Robins Stump

Photo By: Alisha Robins Stump

Boosting the Mind's Eye

Photo By: Alisha Robins Stump

Boosting the Mind's Eye

Photo By: Alisha Robins Stump

Boosting the Mind's Eye

Photo By: Alisha Robins Stump

Photo By: Alisha Robins Stump

Appendix 3:
Social Scene Photos

Part I:

Happy
Play
Love
Affection

Boosting the Mind's Eye

Photo By: Alisha Robins Stump

BOOSTING THE MIND'S EYE

Photos By: Alisha Robins Stump

BOOSTING THE MIND'S EYE

Photos By: Alisha Robins Stump

BOOSTING THE MIND'S EYE

Photo By: Alisha Robins Stump

Photo By: Alisha Robins Stump

BOOSTING THE MIND'S EYE

Photos By: Alisha Robins Stump

Photo By: Alisha Robins Stump

Photo By: Alisha Robins Stump

Photo By: Alisha Robins Stump

Photo By: Alisha Robins Stump

BOOSTING THE MIND'S EYE

Photo By: Steve Visneau

BOOSTING THE MIND'S EYE

Photo By: Steve Visneau

Photo By: Steve Visneau

Photo By: Steve Visneau

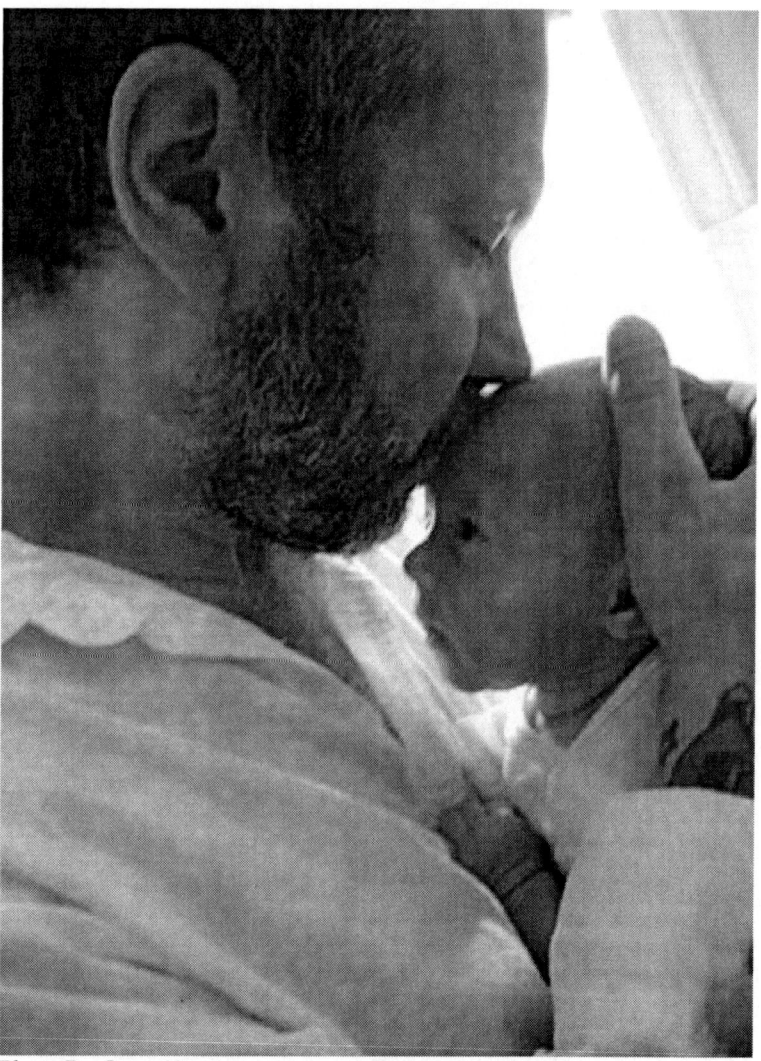

Photo By: Steve Visneau

BOOSTING THE MIND'S EYE

Photo By: Steve Visneau

Boosting the Mind's Eye

Photo By: Steve Visneau

Part II:

Irritation
Upset
Angry
Conflict
Competition

Boosting the Mind's Eye

Photos By: Alisha Robins Stump

Boosting the Mind's Eye

Photo By: Steve Visneau

Photo By: Steve Visneau

Boosting the Mind's Eye

Photo By: Steve Visneau

Boosting the Mind's Eye

Photo By: Steve Visneau

BOOSTING THE MIND'S EYE

Photo By: Steve Visneau

Boosting the Mind's Eye

Photo By: Steve Visneau

BOOSTING THE MIND'S EYE

Photo By: Steve Visneau

Photo By: Steve Visneau

BOOSTING THE MIND'S EYE

Photo By: Steve Visneau

BOOSTING THE MIND'S EYE

Photo By: Steve Visneau

BOOSTING THE MIND'S EYE

Photo By: Steve Visneau

Photo By: Alisha Robins Stump

BOOSTING THE MIND'S EYE

Photo By: Steve Visneau

Boosting the Mind's Eye

Photo By: Steve Visneau

Part III:

Empathy
Sympathy
Concern
Comfort
Helpful

Boosting the Mind's Eye

Photo By: Alisha Robins Stump

BOOSTING THE MIND'S EYE

Photo By: Alisha Robins Stump

Photos By: Alisha Robins Stump

Photos By: Alisha Robins Stump

Photos By: Alisha Robins Stump

BOOSTING THE MIND'S EYE

Photo By: Alisha Robins Stump

Part IV:

Social Scenes Open for Interpretation

BOOSTING THE MIND'S EYE

Photo By: Steve Visneau

Boosting the Mind's Eye

Photo By: Steve Visneau

BOOSTING THE MIND'S EYE

Photo By: Steve Visneau

Photo By: Steve Visneau

Boosting the Mind's Eye

Photo By: Steve Visneau

373

BOOSTING THE MIND'S EYE

Photo By: Alisha Robins Stump

Appendix 4:

Social Stories

Contents:

Story 1: Family's Stressful Day
Story 2: An Embarrassed Child
Story 3: A Frustrated Dad
Story 4: Making Friends
Story 5: The Broken Leg and the Empathetic Friend
Story 6: Frustration at School
Story 7: Feeling Sad and Angry

Story 1: A Family's Stressful Day

It was a hot July day, and today was moving day. The whole family had their share of work to do. Billy, the big brother, had to move many boxes into the truck. Sally, the little sister, was supposed to vacuum the carpets as the rooms were emptied. Mom and Dad were moving furniture and boxes. Everyone was tired and grumpy.

Sally accidentally ran into Billy while she was vacuuming and he dropped a box with picture frames inside. CRASH!!!! The glass inside the box shattered. Billy was so angry that his face turned red and he balled up his fists and yelled, "SALLY! How could you do this? Now, all of Mom and Dad's pictures are ruined and it's all your fault! You are going to be in so much trouble!" Sally cried, "I'm sorry, Billy. I didn't see you, it was an accident. Please don't tell Mom and Dad that it was all MY fault!"

Billy stomped off to tattle to Mom and Dad. Mom and Dad walked into the room and saw that Sally had been crying. Dad put his arms around her and said, "It's ok Sally. We know it was an accident. Let's try and be more careful." Mom turned to Billy and stated, "Billy, you need to learn to control your temper. It is not nice to yell at your sister. You really hurt her feelings. I believe you owe her an apology."

Billy looked at his sister and quickly said, "I'm sorry." Dad said to everyone, "The important thing is that we all get along. Although we are tired and grouchy from the hard work, it does not give us the right to take it out on each other. Why don't we take a break and go get some ice cream? I think we all deserve a little treat."

Questions:

1) How could Billy have handled that differently?
2) Why did Sally cry? Would you have? What would you have said to Billy?
3) Do you think that Billy's parents should have said something about his temper? Why? What would you have said to Billy?
4) Why did Billy yell at his sister? What was he the most worried about? Do you think he was worried he'd get into trouble?
5) Do you think tattling is a good or bad thing? Why?
6) Why is it important to treat each other well even when things are hard? How might this be difficult? What are some ways to help stay calm when everyone is tired and stressed?

Story 2: An Embarrassed Child

Sally was in the 4th grade and did not look forward to going to school. She felt that she didn't fit in with the rest of the kids. She had trouble reading and felt embarrassed when asked to read aloud in the classroom. Mrs. Hinkley, her teacher, was nice, but didn't seem to listen to Sally when she told her how she felt.

One day, Sally was called on in class to read a paragraph aloud from their history book. Her faced blushed and turned bright red. All of the other kids began to giggle at her. She overheard Johnny teasing, "Look at Sally! She looks like a turnip! I can't wait to hear her read. This should take all day!" The other kids laughed at Johnny's comment, but Mrs. Hinkley told Johnny that he was to stay after class so she could speak with him.

Sally smiled a little knowing that Johnny got into trouble. And yet, she couldn't get rid of the giant knot inside of her stomach. She still had to read in front of everyone and just knew that she would make mistakes! Sally began to read very slowly, no one made a sound. She felt better as everyone was quiet and began to feel a little more comfortable. She began to read a little faster and was able to correct herself as she went. When she finished the page, she looked up at Mrs. Hinkley, who was smiling brightly at Sally. "Great job, Sally! Your reading sounds really nice. I can tell you've been working hard."

After that, Sally felt better about her reading. She was glad Mrs. Hinkley complimented her reading and stood up for her when she felt embarrassed.

Questions:

1) Why was Sally embarrassed to read in front of others?
2) How do you think Sally felt at the beginning of the story when Mrs. Hinkley didn't listen to her feelings about reading?
3) Do you think Mrs. Hinkley understood how Sally felt about reading? Why or why not? What behaviors showed that she did or did not?
4) What would you have said to Johnny if he had made fun of you in class?
5) Have you ever felt embarrassed at school? What was the situation and how did you react to others? What would you have done differently?
6) Role play this scenario and take turns playing Sally, Johnny, and Mrs. Hinkley. Describe your feelings after playing each character. How does each character feel different?

Story 3: A Frustrated Dad

David wanted to play outside, but Dad said that before he could, he must complete his homework. David was in the 3rd grade and groaned at the thought. He really did not like doing his homework because he had a hard time understanding what he read.

Dad always helped him with his homework, but sometimes became frustrated with David. So, they sat down together at the kitchen table and began working on David's reading homework. He was asked to read a story and then answer some questions after the story. David began to read the story aloud. He was a really good reader and never seemed to miss a word! David's dad smiled at him while he listened along.

After David read the story, his dad took the book and began to ask him questions about the passage. David was supposed to answer the questions aloud and then write his answers on paper. His father asked, "What happened to Greg after they reached the castle?" David looked at his father and said, "I don't remember." David's father asked, "How can you not remember? You just read the passage...Here, read this part again."

David reread the part that answered the question. His father asked him the same question again. David hung his head and said, "I don't know Dad. I get confused about that part." David's father replied, "I just don't think you were listening. You are going to sit here and reread this story until you get all of these questions right."

David felt very nervous and sad because he knew that he would get many of the questions wrong. He did not feel capable of reading the story and answering the questions. He knew his dad would be disappointed with him. David sat alone at the table for 2 hours working on his homework. He had only finished 3 out of the 10 questions. He began to cry softly and his father heard him from the other room. He came in and said, "What's wrong David? Why haven't you completed your homework? Why are you making this so difficult?"

David replied, "Dad, I really don't understand this and I think that I'm just dumb or something!" His dad said, "David, you're not dumb at all! I think that maybe we need to go speak with your teacher and school counselor and see if you can get some extra help. How does that sound?" David replied, "Thanks Dad. I am just so worried that you don't think I'm trying." His father hugged David and apologized for getting angry with him. He realized that David was trying very hard, but needed some extra help.

Questions:

1) Why do you think David's dad became upset with David?
2) How do you think David felt when his dad became angry with him?
3) Why did David begin to cry?
4) How do you think David felt when his father told him that he would get him some extra help with his reading?
5) What do you think happened after this story? Give your own ending to this story.
6) How would you have reacted if you were David? What type of feelings might you have had?
7) Role play each of the characters and describe your feelings after each turn.

Story 4: Making Friends

Ellen was in the 3rd grade. She did not like school because she did not seem to have any friends. Every day, she tried to talk to the girls during lunch, but they always teased her, or walked away. She felt so sad because she was lonely and wanted friends to talk to and play with during recess.

One day, during math class, Ellen was supposed to be listening to her math teacher, but she could not pay attention. She began to worry about lunchtime and how the girls would tease her, or would not play with her. Ellen was short for her age and wore glasses. She just knew that everyone hated her because she looked ugly. What was she going to do for lunch? Where would she go? She did not want to be teased again – she just couldn't take it! It made her feel so sad and yucky that she was not ever able to eat her lunch.

Her teacher, Mr. Ortiz, saw her worrying as he was giving the math lesson. After math was over, he called Ellen over to his desk.

"Ellen, why do you look so sad today?" Mr. Ortiz asked.

"It's nothing, really," she fibbed.

"I don't believe that Ellen. Everyday during the math lesson, you begin to look sad and worried. I am concerned about you. Talk to me so that I can help you" Mr. Ortiz said.

Ellen began to cry, "I hate school! Everyday at lunchtime, the girls tease me and I just don't have any friends! I know that I am ugly and no one likes me."

Mr. Ortiz handed Ellen a tissue. "It is so hard to be different from the other kids. When I was your age, I use to have to wear leg braces because of the way I walked. All of the kids made fun of me and I had no friends. But, one day, I realized that part of the reason I had no friends was because I had such a poor opinion of myself. I thought that I was ugly, but that was just not true. So, one day, I decided to do a little experiment. I went to school and smiled and said hello to everyone I saw. Even if they were mean to me and said mean things, I smiled at them and said hello to them anyway. Do you know what happened?"

Ellen looked at him with big, bright eyes. "What?"

"I made two new friends that day. Two people said hello to me and came up and talked to me. They said that they didn't talk to me before because I was always frowning and they thought that I didn't want anyone around me. So, you see? My face told people to leave me alone because I looked so sad. Some people even thought I was mean! Can you believe it? Here I was sad and lonely and some people saw my face as mean and wanting to be left alone."

"That is crazy! That is definitely not what is happening to me! I have tried talking to the girls, but they won't have anything to do with me!" Ellen sobbed.

"I know you are hurting right now and how hard it is to feel alone all of the time. But, maybe, you can think about what I said and give it a try sometime," Mr. Ortiz said.

Ellen looked at him, "I guess. But I don't see how that will help."

That day after school, Ellen went home and thought about Mr. Ortiz's story. That couldn't have been true! So, she decided that she was going to prove him wrong and try out his idea the very next day. She knew that it wouldn't work, but she also knew that she had tried everything she knew to do and still felt so lonely. Ellen would give anything to have some friends at school.

The next day, Ellen woke up, looked in the mirror and told herself that she would look people in their eyes, smile, and say hello to the boys and girls at school. She might even smile at the teachers too! She felt excited about this new outlook on her day. She dressed herself in her favorite jeans and sweater and even put a new bow in her hair. She was really going to look great today!

When she got to school, she felt butterflies in her stomach, which she knew meant that she was nervous. She took a deep breath and began to walk towards her classroom. She kept her head up and looked others in the eye as she walked by. She smiled and said, "Good morning!" to everyone she saw. Some smiled back and said good morning too! This was amazing! She had no idea that others would ever smile at her. She walked into her classroom and smiled at Mr. Ortiz. She said good morning to him as well! He smiled back and told her good morning too. This was turning out to be quite the experiment.

During her math lesson, Ellen began to feel a little nervous about lunchtime. What if the girls didn't talk to her? What if they laughed at her? Then, she pushed those thoughts aside and told herself that as long as she was smiling and being nice to people she was making her best effort at making new friends.

When the bell rang for lunchtime, Ellen kept her head high and walked to the cafeteria. After getting her lunch tray, Ellen walked up to a group of girls sitting down. She looked them in the eye and said very nicely, "Would you mind if I sat down with you?" The girls nodded "Yes." So, Ellen smiled and sat down with her tray. She began to eat and listen to their conversation. They talked about class, movies, and boys that were in their class. Ellen felt so comfortable that after a while, she realized that she had joined in the conversation as well! She didn't even realize that she had begun to speak, but she had. The girls didn't make fun of her or even tell her to be quiet. By the end of lunch, all of the girls were laughing and enjoying themselves. Ellen knew that this was the start of a whole new school experience for her. That morning she had been so sure that Mr. Ortiz's experiment wouldn't have worked, but it did!

After school, Ellen thanked Mr. Ortiz for his suggestion and told him of her day. She went home smiling and excited for the next day of school. She couldn't wait to tell her parents the great news that she had made new friends!

Questions:

1) Why do you think Ellen thought that she was ugly?
2) How do you think Ellen's behavior changed that allowed her to make friends?
3) Why do you think Mr. Ortiz told Ellen that story?
4) Why was Ellen so happy at the end of the story?
5) Do you think all of Ellen's problems are solved? Why or why not?
6) How would you have handled that situation if you were Ellen? Would you have tried Mr. Ortiz's experiment? Why or why not?
7) Why is it important that people not tease others that are different? How does it make people feel when others are mean to them? Why?
8) Have you ever been teased by your classmates? What did you do when they were mean to you?

Story 5: The Empathetic Friend

Summer was supposed to be the best time ever; but, not for Jimmy. He broke his leg playing basketball and would have to spend the rest of the summer in a cast. He was so sad and frustrated as he watched his friends ride on their bikes and head to the local swimming pool. What was he going to do all summer? He really didn't like watching TV all that much, reading was too much like homework, and he just knew his baby sister was going to drive him bananas!

One morning when Jimmy woke up, he heard a tapping at his bedroom window. He hopped his way over to the window to find his friend, Bruce smiling widely at him.

"How are you this fine morning?" Bruce asked with a smile.

"What are you so happy about? This is not a fine morning for me; I'm stuck in this stupid cast." Jimmy complained.

"Well, I have a great idea and I wanted to surprise you. So, get dressed and meet me at your front door." Bruce replied.

Jimmy got dressed quickly and couldn't help but wonder what his best friend Bruce had up his sleeve. He and Bruce had been best friends since they were babies. He could have sworn that Bruce had baseball camp all summer, so Jimmy couldn't understand why he was here at his house this morning.

Jimmy made his way to the front door with his crutches. He had gotten pretty good on these things and could whip around quickly! He opened the door and saw that Bruce had this big cooler in his arms. He also had 2 fishing poles and a wagon attached to the back of his bike!

"What is that?" asked Jimmy in surprise.

"That is your ride, King Jimmy. Hop aboard, we are going fishing for the day and going to have a great time!" Bruce said.

Jimmy got into the wagon with hesitation. He was a little worried that Bruce was going to run the wagon off the road with his bike. But, he trusted his best friend and knew that he would be extra careful.

The boys spent the day fishing at their favorite fishing spot along the lake. Bruce had even made Jimmy's favorite ham and cheese sandwiches for lunch. Jimmy had a great time and was so thankful to have a friend like Bruce.

"I thought you had baseball camp this summer," Jimmy said.

"I did, but I thought that I would have more fun hanging out with you. Besides, I can do baseball camp anytime. How often do you get to spend time with your best friend and do fun stuff like fishing?" Bruce replied.

Jimmy couldn't believe it! Bruce had blown off baseball camp just to hang out with him.

"Bruce, I don't want you to miss camp for me. You are a really good catcher this year. You should be practicing and getting better for next season." Jimmy said.

"Naaa...I talked to my parents about it and they thought it was a great idea to take a break. Besides, this way I can play baseball for the summer league and just have some fun. You can come watch my games." Bruce said.

"I don't know what to say, Bruce. You are a good friend to do that for me. I was really sad this summer because I thought it was going to be so boring, but now I know that we are going to have a great time!" Jimmy said with excitement.

"Sometimes, you just have to figure out what's important. What could be more important than a best friend?" Bruce said with a smile.

Questions:

1) Why do you think Jimmy was sad when he found out he was going to have to spend his summer indoors?
2) Why do you think Bruce quit baseball camp?
3) Do you think Bruce's friendship was more important to him than camp? Why?
4) What would you have done if your best friend was hurt for the summer? Why?
5) How would you feel if you were Jimmy and your best friend made that type of sacrifice for you?
6) Tell about a time when you made a sacrifice for someone you love.
7) Imagine a time that you might be able to make a sacrifice for someone and describe that situation.

Story 6: Frustration at School

Hilary was in the 6th grade. She knew that she was supposed to enjoy school because everyone around her seemed happy to be there. Other children smiled while they did their work, or laughed on the playground; but, not Hilary. She hated school. She wished that she would never have to go to school again. School was okay when she was in the first, second, and third grades, but the day she started 4th grade, she knew that she was in trouble. She would often go home and cry to her mom and dad about how hard school was and how much work they gave her.

Mom and Dad listened to her, hugged her, and offered to help her with her homework, but it didn't help. Nothing seemed to help. She just could not seem to remember the information she read. She worked hard every night to read and memorize the material for the next day's test, but it didn't matter. As soon as it was time for the test, she had forgotten everything she had read. She just knew that she was dumb and she would never amount to anything. Her parents talked about her being a doctor one day, but Hilary could barely remember anything about science or math. How would she ever be smart enough to go to medical school?

As Hilary's alarm clock beeped loudly on her bedside table, Hilary slowly sat up and turned it off. "Great, another day of school," Hilary thought as she slowly walked to the bathroom to wash her face. She had a horrible feeling in her stomach. As she dressed and went downstairs, her mother greeted her with pancakes.

"I made your favorite, Hilary! Blueberry pancakes." Her mother beamed.

"No thanks, Mom. I'm not hungry. I'll see you after school." Hilary said with a heavy voice.

Hilary's mom came around to her and hugged her close.

"I love you, Hilary and just want you to be happy. What

can I do to help?" Her mom asked.

"Nothing, Mom. I will figure it out. I'll be fine, honest." Hilary lied.

As Hilary walked to school, she realized that maybe she did need some help, but she didn't want to bother her parents with her problems. Plus, she didn't want her parents to worry about her and think that she couldn't succeed. Hilary decided that she would go talk to Ms. Robins, the school counselor that morning.

Hilary waited for Ms. Robins outside of her office. She didn't know what to say to her, but hoped that she would figure it out once she spoke with her. Ms. Robins opened the door and asked Hilary to come in and sit down.

"Hilary, I am so glad that you decided to come in and see me. I have been meaning to meet with you." Ms. Robins said.

"You have? What for?" Hilary asked.

"Well, I have noticed that your grades have been slipping and I wanted to talk with you about that." Ms. Robins said.

"Yeah. I have been having some problems with my school work. It has gotten really hard for me and I can't seem to remember anything when it's time to take the test."

"You know, I had the same problem when I was in school. I know just the person who can help you. Her name is Ms. Collins and she is a learning specialist who helps kids make pictures in their head. It really helps them remember what they read." Ms. Robins said.

"Really? I can't believe that! That seems too easy. Do you think she'll meet with me?" Hilary asked with excitement.

"I'm sure we can arrange a time for you two to start working together. Let me make the arrangements and I will let you know by the end of the school day." Ms. Robins said.

"Thank you, Ms. Robins! That would be great." Hilary beamed.

Hilary went to class that morning with a new found

enthusiasm. Could Ms. Collins really help her? She sure hoped so, that would make life so much easier! How great it would be if school were easier, then she could focus on having more fun and making new friends. She just didn't have much time for socializing these days because she was always studying.

Ms. Robins called Hilary into her office after school. Ms. Collins was there and seemed so happy to meet Hilary.

"I have heard so many nice things about you, Hilary." Ms. Collins said. "I would really like to start working with you during your English hour. Ms. Robins has worked it out with your teacher so that you can come to my office. How does that sound to you?"

"That sounds really good. I would like to learn a new way to remember my school work. It has gotten hard lately and I have not really wanted to come to school. I feel as though I should just quit because no matter how hard I try, I can't seem to get good grades." Hilary replied with sadness.

"I know just how you feel. I see so many students with the same feelings. It is ok to feel sad and frustrated. You are a smart girl, but you just need a new way to think about what you learn. There is nothing wrong with that." Ms. Collins explained.

"It is nice to know that I am not the only student with this problem. When do we start?" Hilary asked.

Hilary began seeing Ms. Collins every day. After two weeks, Hilary started to sense that school wasn't so bad after all. She was able to remember more and not have to try so hard when learning in school. Hilary also realized that she was able to understand the teacher when she spoke. Before, she always wished the teacher would slow down when she talked because she couldn't understand her very well. Now, she was able to keep up in class and with her homework.

Hilary's alarm clock beeped loudly on her bedside table, she hopped out of bed with a smile on her face. She was excited to go to school and see all of her friends. She had just aced her math test the day before and was so proud of herself! This was going to be her last day with Ms. Collins. She was sad about not seeing her anymore, but happy that she didn't need to have special tutoring. She was able to do her school work on her own and make good grades!

Hilary bounded down the stairs. Her mother met her with blueberry pancakes. Hilary ate them with a smile and headed off to school. Today was going to be a great day!

Questions:

1) Why did Hilary not like going to school at the beginning of the story?
2) Why do you think that Hilary was so sad and lacking in energy at the beginning of the story? Have you ever felt that way? Why?
3) How did Hilary's feelings about school change? Why?
4) Have you ever experienced the feelings that Hilary did in this story? What do you believe caused those feelings?
5) How did Ms. Robins and Ms. Collins help Hilary? Why do you think they wanted to help her?
6) Do you think that Hilary will be able to go onto medical school?
7) Why did Hilary not want to talk about her feelings with her parents? Do you think this was a good choice? Have you ever felt that way? Describe.

Story 7: Feeling Sad and Angry

Orlando started his first day of High School. He was very nervous and scared because this was such a big change from Jr. High – the school was bigger, there were more kids, and everyone knew that the classes were so much harder. Orlando walked into his first class, geometry, and everyone stared as he took his seat. Orlando felt himself getting red as the other kids stared at him.

He never felt like he fit in because he was so much shorter than the rest of the guys his age. He hadn't grown much taller in years, so he was almost a whole head shorter than the girls his age. It was really embarrassing and often difficult for Orlando to feel comfortable around other kids his age. So, he often kept to himself because he knew that no one really wanted to be his friend. He was worried that he would spend this year like the last, lonely and without any friends. Orlando settled into his seat and tried to focus on the math teacher's lecture.

When Orlando walked home that day after school, he immediately went into his room and talked to no one. He didn't want to tell his mom what a bad day he'd had at school. She was always trying to cheer him up and make him feel better. He was lucky because he had a mom that loved him so much, but sometimes, her love was more than he could stand. He didn't want to make her sad with his own problems.

Orlando sat alone in his room feeling really depressed. Sometimes he just didn't want to deal with life anymore. He felt that he would just be better off going to sleep. Just then, his mom knocked on the door.

"Orlando? You in there?" she asked.

"Yeah, Mom. I'm here, but I want to be left alone right now, okay?" Orlando replied.

Orlando's mom could sense the sadness in his voice. She was really worried about him and wanted to find him someone to talk to. He would no longer talk with her and his father did not live with them any longer. Orlando's relationship with his father was not very close and she knew Orlando needed someone to confide in and share his feelings. Orlando's mom slowly opened his door and found him laying on the floor listening to sad music.

"Orlando...I've been thinking. Last year was really tough on you and I was hoping that this year would be a fresh start for you at the High School. But, I can see that your first day looked pretty rough. I was hoping to make a suggestion that you might find helpful." She said.

"What now Mom? I am just not up for talking about it, ok?" Orlando mumbled.

"I know and I'm not asking you to talk with me about it. But, I have found someone that I think you would be more comfortable talking to. His name is Dr. Henley and he is a therapist who can help you to work through some of your feelings." She said.

"A shrink! Are you kidding Mom? I'm not crazy! I don't need some doctor drugging me up and asking me how I feel about everything. That is crazy! No way!" Orlando yelled.

"I understand you may think that doctors are only for people that are 'crazy,' but I assure you that many sane people have gone to therapists. Sometimes we just get stuck and need a little nudge in the right direction. I am not forcing you to go, but I am strongly urging that you do. I am giving you his card and ask that you call him yourself. That way, you both can decide if you are 'crazy' enough to go," Orlando's mom said with a grin.

"Thanks Mom...Now, you think I'm crazy?" he said with a smile.

"I sure do! You're related to me aren't you? Everyone in this town knows that I'm a nut!" She laughed.

Orlando and his mom had dinner and were able to discuss his day. He felt better already, but knew that going to school the next day would create the same feelings of sadness and anger he felt earlier. Maybe he would call Dr.

Henley, just to see... Who knows? Maybe the guy could help him figure out how to grow 5 inches!

Orlando had a bad day the following day at school. Kids teased him about his height; he retreated, and talked with no one. He walked home feeling deflated and hurt. He could not take this for another year! He knew that the sadness and anger would be too much for him to deal with alone. When he got home, he decided that he would call Dr. Henley. Maybe he had some suggestions about how to deal with the teasing at school.

He called Dr. Henley and made an appointment with his secretary. He was really proud of himself and walked into the kitchen and told his Mom the day of the appointment. They put it on the family calendar, so no one would forget.

The day of the appointment, Orlando felt better already. He knew that Dr. Henley was going to help him. "Plus, the doctor couldn't make fun of his height, it was unprofessional, right?" Orlando thought to himself.

Orlando waited his turn at Dr. Henley's office and was finally called back for his appointment. His mom waited for him in the waiting room and smiled her best smile as he walked towards the doctor's office. Orlando met Dr. Henley, a tall handsome man. Immediately, Orlando felt very short and ugly. Maybe this wasn't such a good idea after all.

"Hello Orlando! I am Dr. Henley. It is very nice to meet you. Please sit down. Today we will talk about what brings you here and how I can best help you. Does that sound okay?"

"Sure," Orlando said with little enthusiasm.

"Why don't you tell me what prompted you to call and make an appointment," Dr. Henley stated.

"Well. Ever since I can remember, I have been the shortest person in my class. Everyone teases me and I can't seem to make any friends. I wish that I didn't have to go to school at all," Orlando replied.

"I can imagine how difficult that must be for you to be the shortest in your class. What type of feelings do you have when people tease you?" the Dr. asked.

"I feel angry, sad, and then I feel ugly and worthless," Orlando said.

"It's good that you can express your feelings; however, those are not the type of emotions anyone wants to feel daily. Maybe we can work through some of your experiences and come up with a solution for dealing with the teasing. How does that sound?" Dr. Henley asked.

"Ok, I guess. But, how is that going to help me feel better. I'm tired of feeling sad and lonely." Orlando replied.

"That must be really difficult to feel those feelings every day. My goal with you will be to work on replacing some of your negative thoughts and feelings about yourself with more positive ones. In this way, you will learn how to deal not only with the teasing, but how to feel good about yourself despite what others say to you. Once you begin feeling better about yourself, you may find yourself making new friends and finding activities that you are interested in. Does this sound like an ok plan to you?" Dr. Henley asked.

"Sure, I guess," Orlando replied softly.

Orlando began seeing Dr. Henley every week. He learned new ways to deal with people who were mean to him, as well as his own feelings about himself. He slowly began to change his behavior when kids teased him. He began to stand up for himself using his humor and not allowing the kids to hurt his feelings. Over time, he noticed that fewer kids teased him because they knew he was not affected by their meanness. Orlando also began making friends and joined the theatre group at school. He was really good at acting and loved playing comedic roles.

His mom was so proud of her son's accomplishments. She knew that Orlando was going to make it and learn how to deal with his issues in a more positive and mature manner. He continued to see Dr. Henley throughout the year, but began seeing him less and less. He no longer needed the weekly sessions in order to do well in school and life.

The biggest surprise came to everyone when Orlando grew 5 inches that very year! Who knew Orlando was not going to be the shortest person in his class? Even though Orlando grew, he knew he would not have been able to deal with others effectively without a little help. He was glad he put effort into seeing Dr. Henley.

Questions:

1) Why did Orlando feel sad and angry after going to school? Would you have felt the same way?
2) What do you think were the most important things for Orlando to learn with Dr. Henley? Do you think he learned those things? Why?
3) How would you handle kids at school teasing you?
4) Do you think Orlando would have been okay with out seeing Dr. Henley because he grew 5 inches? Why or why not?
5) What do you think are the most important lessons to learn while you are in school?
6) Why do you believe that it is important to make friends and feel accepted in school? Do you think this affects how people feel about themselves? Why?
7) What would you have done if you were Orlando and experiencing his problems? Would you have listened to your mom and seen Dr. Henley? Why or why not?

Appendix 5:
Emotional Discrepancies

BOOSTING THE MIND'S EYE

1) The girl cried as the baby kissed her face.

2) The Mom was so mad that she gave everyone ice cream for dessert.

3) The Dad showed his gratitude by turning and walking away.

4) The child became frustrated when the homework was too easy for her.

5) The old woman smiled as she stubbed her toe on the table.

6) When the little boy started to laugh, the father yelled at him for being so loud.

7) Molly cried as her mother told her that she was getting a new puppy.

8) Sometimes Emily had trouble sleeping because she stopped worrying about her day.

9) Adam remembered how much fun he had at the amusement park and decided he never wanted to go again.

10) As the tears ran down her face, Madison realized that feeling sad was better than any other feeling.

11) Being angry was hard for Eric as he would often laugh every time he felt mad.

12) As Lexi crawled into bed with her book, she felt scared about tomorrow's test. Luckily, she hadn't studied at all.

13) As the roller coaster slowly scooted up the track, Jose felt calm when the roller coaster tipped over the hill and

raced down the track.

14) Robert wanted to ask Mary to the dance, but felt too confident to ask her out.

15) Stacy cared for her roommate, but decided that she did not want to remain friends because she liked her too much.

16) Karen and Fred were very much in love. You can tell because whenever they were together, they often scowled at one another.

17) Kelly loved her dog so much that she yelled at her every day.

18) Whenever Ryan wanted to express his frustration with his sister, he often made it a point not to call her for at least a month.

19) Mike loved his family so much that he spent a lot of time away from them.

20) Jack knew that life was short, so he spent many a happy moment criticizing those around him.

21) John was so proud of his son, Joe, who did not graduate from high school.

22) Cecilia wanted to feel good about herself, so she went shopping because she knew that new clothes would make it all better.
23) Mitch always knew how other people around him felt, so he never bothered to ask about people's feelings.

24) Amy sensed that her sister was sad, so she told her that her dog died because she was already feeling sad

anyway.

25) When the boy tripped and fell in the cafeteria, the teacher laughed at him because it was funny.

26) Nicky never asked for help because she knew how to do everything herself.

27) Claudia lied to her mother about where she was going, but her mother smiled because she knew the truth.

28) Sometimes Joanna needed to be left alone, so she called all of her friends to come over and hang out.

29) Simon could not decide who to take to the summer dance, so he flipped a coin to be fair to both of the girls.

30) Katie was really good at skateboarding, but she did not tell anyone because she was embarrassed that others would tease her.

Notes

Chapter 1

[1] Greenspan, S.I. (1997). The Growth of the Mind: And the endangered origins of intelligence. Da Capo Press, p. 125.

[2] Wilford, S. & Karas, E (2005). Understanding the Theory of Multiple Intelligences. *Early Childhood Today, 20(3),* 16-32.

[3] Sternberg, R.J. (2003). *Cognitive Psychology.* (3rd ed.). Belmont, CA: Thomson-Wadsworth.

[4] Grewel, D. & Salovey, P. (2005). Feeling smart: The science of emotional intelligence. American Scientist, 93, 330-339.

Chapter 2

[1] Grewel, D. & Salovey, P. (2005). Feeling smart: The science of emotional intelligence. American Scientist, 93, 330-339.

[2] Mayer, J., Salovey, P., & Caruso, D. (2004). Emotional Intelligence: Theory, Findings, and Implications. *Psychological Inquiry, 15(3),* 197-215. Specific quotes from p. 197 & 198.

[3] Salovey, P., & Pizarro, D.A., (2003). The value of emotional intelligence. In R. J. Sternberg, J. Lautrey, & T. Lubart (Eds.), *Models of Intelligence: International Perspectives* (pp.263-278). Washington, DC: American Psychological Association.

[4] Sternberg, R.J. (2003). *Cognitive Psychology.* (3rd ed.). Belmont, CA: Thomson-Wadsworth.

[5] Caruso, D., Mayer, J., Salovey, P. (2002). Relation of an ability measure of emotional intelligence to personality. *Journal of Personality Assessment, 79(2)*, 306–320.

[6] Elfenbein, H. (2006). Learning in emotion judgments: Training and the cross-cultural understanding of facial expressions. *Journal of Nonverbal Behavior, 30(1)*, p. 21-36. Quote from p. 22.

Chapter 3

[1] Paivio, A. (1991). Dual coding theory: Retrospect and current status. *Canadian Journal of Psychology, 45(3)*, 255-287.

[2] Sadoski, M., Goetz, E., Kealy, W., & Paivio, A. (1997). Concreteness and imagery effects in the written composition of definitions. *Journal of Educational Psychology, 89(3)*, 518-526.

[3] Mazoyer, B., Tzourio-Mazoyer, N., & Mazard, A., Denis, M., & Mellet, E. (2002). Neural bases of image and language interactions. *International Journal of Psychology, 37 (4)*, 204–208.

[4] Kounios, J. & Holcomb, P. (1994). Concreteness Effects in Semantic Processing: ERP Evidence Supporting Dual-Coding Theory. *Journal of Experimental Psychology: Learning, Memory, and Cognition, 20(4)*, 804-823.

[5] *Lindamood-Bell Research* (2004). Retrieved from http://www.lindamoodbell.com/downloads/pdf/research/SS%20Stats%20'05.pdf on September 15, 2006.

[6] Sadoski, M. (2001). Resolving the effects of concreteness on interest, comprehension, and learning important ideas from text. *Educational Psychology, 13(3)*, 263-281.

[7] Reed, S.K. (2006). Cognitive architectures for multimedia learning. *Educational Psychologist, 41(2), 87-98.* Retrieved from Academic Search Premier.

[8] Whitehead, D. (2001). Parallels between dual coding theory and quantum physics. *Encounter: Education for Meaning and Social Justice, 14(3), 42-47.* Retrieved from Academic Search Premier.

Chapter 4

[1] www.lindamoodbell.com

[2] Grewel, D. & Salovey, P. (2005). Feeling smart: The science of emotional intelligence. *American Scientist, 93,* 330-339.

[3] Trauner, D. A., Ballantyne, A., Chase, D., & Tallal, P. (1993). Comprehension and expression of affect in language-impaired children. *Journal of Psycholinguistic Research, 22(4),* 445-452.

[4] Merton, R. K. (1965). On the Shoulders of Giants: A Shandean Postscript. New York: Free Press.

[5] Sadoski, M. (2001). Resolving the effects of concreteness on interest, comprehension, and learning important ideas from text. *Educational Psychology, 13(3),* 263-281.

[6] Whitehouse, A.J.O., Mayberry, M.T., Durkin, K. (2006). Inner speech impairments in autism. *Journal of Child Psychology and Psychiatry, 47(8),* 857-865.

Chapter 5

[1] Duke, M.P., Nowicky, S., & Martin, E.A. (1996). *Teaching Your Child the Language of Social Success*. Atlanta: Peachtree.

[2] Salovey, P., & Pizarro, D.A., (2003). The value of emotional intelligence. In R. J. Sternberg, J. Lautrey, & T. Lubart (Eds.), *Models of Intelligence: International Perspectives* (pp.263-278). Washington, DC: American Psychological Association.

Chapter 7

[1] Paivio, A. (2007). *Mind and Its Evolution: A dual coding theoretical approach*. New Jersey: Lawrence Erlbaum Associates.

[2] Igo, L.B., Kiewra, K.A., & Burning, R. (2004). Removing the snare from the pair: Using pictures to learn confusing word pairs. *The Journal of Experimental Education, 72(3)*, 165-178.

[3] Sadoski, M. (2001). Resolving the effects of concreteness on interest, comprehension, and learning important ideas from text. *Educational Psychology, 13(3)*, 263-281.

Chapter 9

[1] Duke, M.P., Nowicky, S., & Martin, E.A. (1996). *Teaching Your Child the Language of Social Success*. Atlanta: Peachtree.

Chapter 11

[1] Roberston, Ian (2002). *Opening the Mind's Eye: How images and language teach us how to see*. New York: St. Martin's Press.

² Goleman, Daniel (2006). *Social Intelligence: The new science of human relationships.* New York: Bantam Books.

Chapter 12

¹ Sternberg, R.J. (2003). *Cognitive Psychology.* (3rd ed.). Belmont, CA: Thomson-Wadsworth.

² Salovey, P., & Pizarro, D.A., (2003). The value of emotional intelligence. In R. J. Sternberg, J. Lautrey, & T. Lubart (Eds.), *Models of Intelligence: International Perspectives* (pp.263-278). Washington, DC: American Psychological Association.

³ Bell, N. (1991). Gestalt imagery: A critical factor in language comprehension. *Annals of Dyslexia, 41,* 246-260.

Chapter 13

¹ Granello, D. H. (2000). Encouraging the Cognitive Development of Supervisees: Using Bloom's Taxonomy in Supervision. *Counselor Education & Supervision, 40,* 31-47.

² Petress, Ken. (2004). Critical Thinking: An Extended Definition. *Education,* 124(3), 461-467.

³ Krumme, G. (2001) *Major Categories in the Taxonomy of Educational Objectives (Bloom 1956).* Retrieved May 2, 2005, from University of Washington, Seattle Web site: http://faculty.washington.edu/krummel/guides/bloom.html

⁴ *Learning Skills Program: Bloom's Taxonomy.* (2003). Retrieved May 2, 2005, from University of Victoria, Counseling Services Web site: www.coun.uvic.ca/learn/programs/hndouts/bloom.html.

Chapter 19

[1] Sue, D.W., & Sue, D. (2003). *Counseling the culturally diverse* (4th Ed.) New York: John Wiley & Sons.

[2] Rosenblum, K.E., & Travis, T.M. (2006). *The meaning of difference: American constructions of race, sex, and gender, social class, and sexual orientation* (4th Ed.) New York: McGraw-Hill.

[3] Interview with Dr. Beverly Greene, n.d. *Issues of Power and Diversity*. Retrieved on April 9, 2007.

Chapter 20

[1] Roberston, Ian (2002). *Opening the Mind's Eye: How images and language teach us how to see.* New York: St. Martin's Press.

[2] Goleman, Daniel (2006). *Social Intelligence: The new science of human relationships.* New York: Bantam Books.

[3] Bennett M.P., Zeller J.M., Rosenberg L., et al. (2003). The effect of mirthful laughter on stress and natural killer cell activity. *Alternative Therapies in Health and Medicine, 9,* 38-45.

References

Bell, N. (1991). Gestalt imagery: A critical factor in language comprehension. *Annals of Dyslexia, 41*, 246-260.

Bennett M.P., Zeller J.M., Rosenberg L., et al. (2003). The effect of mirthful laughter on stress and natural killer cell activity. *Alternative Therapies in Health and Medicine, 9*, 38-45.

Caruso, D., Mayer, J., Salovey, P. (2002). Relation of an ability measure of emotional intelligence to personality. *Journal of Personality Assessment, 79(2)*, 306–320.

Duke, M.P., Nowicky, S., & Martin, E.A. (1996). *Teaching Your Child the Language of Social Success.* Atlanta: Peachtree.

Elfenbein, H. (2006). Learning in emotion judgments: Training and the cross-cultural understanding of facial expressions. *Journal of Nonverbal Behavior, 30(1)*, p. 21-36.

Goleman, Daniel (1995). *Emotional Intelligence: Why it can matter more than IQ.* New York: Bantam Books.

Goleman, Daniel (2006). *Social Intelligence: The new science of human relationships.* New York: Bantam Books.

Granello, D. H. (2000). Encouraging the Cognitive Development of Supervisees: Using Bloom's Taxonomy in Supervision. *Counselor Education & Supervision*, 40, 31-47.

Greenspan, S.I. (1997). *The Growth of the Mind: And the endangered origins of intelligence.* Da Capo Press.

Grewel, D. & Salovey, P. (2005). Feeling smart: The science of emotional intelligence. *American Scientist, 93,* 330-339.

Igo, L.B., Kiewra, K.A., & Burning, R. (2004). Removing the snare from the pair: Using pictures to learn confusing word pairs. *The Journal of Experimental Education, 72(3),* 165-178.

Interview with Dr. Beverly Greene, n.d. *Issues of Power and Diversity.* Retrieved on April 9, 2007.

Kounios, J. & Holcomb, P. (1994). Concreteness Effects in Semantic Processing: ERP Evidence Supporting Dual-Coding Theory. *Journal of Experimental Psychology: Learning, Memory, and Cognition, 20(4),* 804-823.

Krumme, G. (2001) *Major Categories in the Taxonomy of Educational Objectives (Bloom 1956).* Retrieved May 2, 2005, from University of Washington, Seattle Web site: http://faculty.washington.edu/krummel/guides/bloom.html

Learning Skills Program: Bloom's Taxonomy. (2003). Retrieved May 2, 2005, from University of Victoria, Counseling Services Web site: www.coun.uvic.ca/learn/programs/hndouts/bloom.html

Lindamood-Bell Research (2004). Retrieved from http://www.lindamoodbell.com/downloads/pdf/research/SS%20Stats%20'05.pdf on September 15, 2006.

Mayer, J., Salovey, P., & Caruso, D. (2004). Emotional Intelligence: Theory, Findings, and Implications. *Psychological Inquiry, 15(3)*, 197-215.

Mazoyer, B., Tzourio-Mazoyer, N., & Mazard, A., Denis, M., & Mellet, E. (2002). Neural bases of image and language interactions. *International Journal of Psychology, 37 (4)*, 204–208.

Merton, R. K. (1965). On the Shoulders of Giants: A Shandean Postscript. New York: Free Press.

Paivio, A. (1991). Dual coding theory: Retrospect and current status. *Canadian Journal of Psychology, 45(3)*, 255-287.

Paivio, A. (2007). *Mind and Its Evolution: A dual coding theoretical approach.* New Jersey: Lawrence Erlbaum Associates.

Petress, Ken. (2004). Critical Thinking: An Extended Definition. *Education*, 124(3), 461-467.

Reed, S.K. (2006). Cognitive architectures for multimedia learning. Educational Psychologist, 41(2), 87-98. Retrieved from Academic Search Premier.

Roberston, Ian (2002). *Opening the Mind's Eye: How images and language teach us how to see.* New York: St. Martin's Press.

Rosenblum, K.E., & Travis, T.M. (2006). *The meaning of difference: American constructions of race, sex, and gender, social class, and sexual orientation* (4th Ed.) New York: McGraw-Hill.

Sadoski, M. (2001). Resolving the effects of concreteness on interest, comprehension, and learning important ideas from text. *Educational Psychology, 13(3),* 263-281.

Sadoski, M., Goetz, E., Kealy, W., & Paivio, A. (1997). Concreteness and imagery effects in the written composition of definitions. *Journal of Educational Psychology, 89(3),* 518-526.

Salovey, P., Brackett, M.A., & Mayer, J.D. (Eds.) (2004). *Emotional Intelligence: Key Readings on the Mayer and Salovey Model.* New York: Dude Publishing.

Salovey, P., & Pizarro, D.A., (2003). The value of emotional intelligence. In R. J. Sternberg, J. Lautrey, & T. Lubart (Eds.), *Models of Intelligence: International Perspectives* (pp.263-278). Washington, DC: American Psychological Association.

Stanley, G. (1997). *The Growth of the Mind.* Da Capo Press.

Sternberg, R.J. (2003). *Cognitive Psychology.* (3rd ed.). Belmont, CA: Thomson-Wadsworth.

Sue, D.W., & Sue, D. (2003). *Counseling the culturally diverse* (4th Ed.) New York: John Wiley & Sons.

Trauner, D. A., Ballantyne, A., Chase, D., & Tallal, P. (1993). Comprehension and expression of affect in language-impaired children. *Journal of Psycholinguistic Research, 22(4),* 445-452.

Whitehouse, A.J.O., Mayberry, M.T., Durkin, K. (2006). Inner speech impairments in autism. *Journal of Child Psychology and Psychiatry, 47(8),* 857-865.

Wilford, S. & Karas, E (2005). Understanding the Theory of Multiple Intelligences. *Early Childhood Today, 20(3),* 16-32.

Additional Resources for Parents & Professionals

Teaching Your Child the Language of Social Success
    By: Marshall P. Duke, Ph.D., Stephen Nowicki, Jr., Ph.D., and Elisabeth A. Martin, M.Ed.

The New Social Story Book
    By: Carol Gray

Comic Strip Conversations
    By: Carol Gray

The Social Skills Picture Book: Teaching play, emotion, and communication to children with Autism
    By: Jed Baker, Ph.D.

Social Skills Training: For children and adolescents with Asperger's Syndrome and social-communication problems
    By: Jed Baker, Ph.D.

Thinking in Pictures: And other reports from my life with Autism
    By: Temple Grandin

Unwritten Rules of Social Relationships: Decoding social mysteries through the unique perspectives of Autism
    By: Dr. Temple Grandin and Sean Barron

Careers for Individuals with Asperger Syndrome and High-Functioning Autism
    By: Temple Grandin and Kate Duffy

Emotional Literacy in the Middle School: A 6-step program to promote social, emotional, and academic learning
By: Marvin, Maurer, M.A., Marc A. Brackett, Ph.D., with Francesca Plain, Ed.D.

Navigating the Social World: A curriculum for individuals with Asperger's Syndrome, High Functioning Autism, and related disorders
By: Jeanette McAfee, M.D.

Helping a Child with Nonverbal Learning Disorders or Asperger's Syndrome
By: Kathryn Stewart, Ph.D.

Life Strategies for Teens Workbook
By: Jay McGraw

Try and Make Me! Simple strategies that turn off the tantrums and create cooperation
By: Ray Levy, Ph.D. & Bill O'Hanlon, M.S., L.M.F.T.

About the Author

Erin M. Phifer, M.A., LPC lives in Allen, TX with her husband, two lovely daughters, dog, cat, and guinea pig. She practices therapy privately offering services to children through adulthood requiring assessment and treatment for learning disorders, as well as social and emotional development. She is currently completing her doctorate in Psychology.

For more information or to contact Erin, visit:
www.erinphifer.com

Printed in the United States
107510LV00001B/1-69/P